You're Pregnant!!

You're Pregnant!!

A guide for the longest nine months of your life

KATHRYN HAMMER

CB

CONTEMPORARY BOOKS

Library of Congress Cataloging-in-Publication Data

Hammer, Kathryn.
    You're pregnant! : a guide for the longest nine months of
your life / Kathryn Hammer.
        p.   cm.
    ISBN 0-8092-3472-6
    1. Pregnancy—Humor.   I. Title.
PN6162.H268   1995
818'.5402—dc20   95-6734
                                                    CIP

Published by Contemporary Books
A division of NTC/Contemporary Publishing Group, Inc.
4255 West Touhy Avenue, Lincolnwood (Chicago), Illinois 60712-1975 U.S.A.
Copyright © 1995 by Kathryn Hammer
Printed in the United States of America
International Standard Book Number: 0-8092-3472-6

00 01 02 03 04 05 QM 24 23 22 21 20 19 18 17 16 15 14 13 12 11 10 9 8 7

For all mothers, especially mine

Is there anything more miraculous, more joyous than the birth of a child? It is in the spirit of gladness, joy, and celebration that I write this book, for if there is a sound of joy, it must surely be laughter.

Contents

Introduction

Why You Need This Book

YOU'RE PREGNANT!

If you're like most expectant mothers, you undoubtedly have in your possession eleventy-ten pregnancy and childbirth manuals, each dog-eared and highlighted. One in every room. You gobble up every word, then follow your husband around the house, scurrying behind him, following him into the bathroom, as you read aloud each earthshaking passage. Had you given such conscientious attention to your textbooks while in school, you would now be a Nobel Prize winner and the reigning champion on "Jeopardy!"

You know everything there is to know about pregnancy. You are informed, aware, in charge. And yet, inexplicably, you continue your frenzied search for more information. Your little voice tells you there's more. It is telling you that you are not getting the whole story.

Listen to your brain. Your little voice is right. There *is* more to this than they're letting on. There *is* a conspiracy of silence. There *is* a Gestational Ministry of Propaganda that controls and parcels out only the Prenatally Correct information it wants you to have—all carefully worded and phrased to *sound* exactly like Actual Real Written-in-Stone Irrefutable Information.

But they never tell you the real scoop.

Something weird happens when you're pregnant. (OK, *a lot* weird happens when you're pregnant.) But of all the weirdness, the most disconcerting part is that *no one acknowledges the weirdness.*

It's as if there's a code of silence prohibiting anyone from telling you what to *really* expect when you're expecting. You are left to feel as if you were the only one ever in the history of the universe to notice that, um, this is all quite bizarre.

No matter what your question or concern, no matter what fears or symptoms you bring to them, the Experts all parrot the same thing, starting with "This is perfectly normal." Like Teddy Ruxpins with Ph.D.s, they just pull the string and repeat one of five lines:

1. This is perfectly normal.
2. Eat small, nutritious meals.
3. Don't overdo.
4. Rapid, excess weight gain can compound this problem.
5. If this problem persists, check with your doctor.

It's not that you don't appreciate the reassurance and standard advice. It's just that . . . *could* you possibly be the only preggo ever to think this is one big cosmic joke? Are you supposed to play along and pretend you don't notice the absurdities? Are you on "Mother Nature's Funniest Home Videos?"

Once, just *once*, instead of being told for the umpteenth time, "That's perfectly normal," you would like someone, somewhere simply to look you straight in the eye and flat out say it: "That's *weird*." Or disgusting. Or hilarious. Anything but normal.

Because it *is* odd! All of it. And it's perfectly normal (there's that word again) to think so. You, who wouldn't think of renting out your upstairs bedroom, are now toting around a *person* inside of you! A boarder, a complete stranger has set up housekeeping inside your body, occupying an internal organ that until now had rarely come up in polite conversation. Normal? Hardly. Commonplace, perhaps. But not normal.

And while it may be comforting to know that it's Perfectly Normal for your belly button to push out like that, wouldn't it be nice if someone just came out and said what you're both thinking? ("Holy moly, woman! You could hang pot holders on that thing!")

Because, eventually, you can only take so much calm, reassuring support before something SNAPS. You need a break from normalcy and mature acceptance and confidence and oneness of being and centeredness and preparedness. You want to vent. Bitch a little. Whine. And that's perfectly normal. ("Normal? *NORMAL?!* Someone *smack* that woman.")

Finally there's a book for *you*, the fun preggos out there, who could never settle for mere "normal" during this, the most incredible, uproarious adventure of your life!

1

Am I Pregnant?

A Quick Explanation of
How These Things Happen

When asking the question "Am I pregnant?" it's always helpful to consider first whether you have engaged in any pregnancy-inducing activities. These activities can be found listed in any junior-high health manual and are frequently updated on daytime TV. Consult your local listings.

Most pregnancy-inducing behavior can be categorized as "Contact with Little Tadpole-Type Organisms." These organisms are known as *spermatozoa*, a Latin word meaning "Surprise!"

Because you cannot see sperm (as they are nicknamed) without a microscope, it is difficult for people with normal vision to know whether or not they have encountered one of these creatures.

Fortunately, Nature (in her wisdom) chose not to give these sperm-creatures legs, knowing they could create a great deal of havoc if allowed to roam free on their own.

So there's little likelihood of a chance encounter with a sperm. Try as they might, sperm simply cannot jump onto you as you walk by. Without legs, they just can't muster sufficient springing action and fall harmlessly to the ground, where they flop and writhe about unnoticed.

So, sperm will generally hitch a ride with someone who can get around a bit more easily and safely. Historically, males have been the vehicle of choice. Sperm will then lie in wait for some opportune moment to travel over to you, unnoticed, such as when you are having sex without a microscope.

There are some other, lesser-known ways that you can become pregnant as well, most of which involve unsavory activities with extraterrestrials or demons. The statistical significance of these occurrences is negligible, however, and should be of no concern unless your symptoms include late-night howling and/or craving raw liver. (For further information, consult the supermarket tabloid section of your library.)

You may be saying that you can't be pregnant because, even though you have had sex, you always used birth control. While this is a good argument, there can be holes in your logic, such as those found when tracing back your supply of condoms to the Arkansas public school system.

SIGNS AND SYMPTOMS: CLUES OR RED HERRINGS?

There are many signs to watch for if you think you may be pregnant. The most obvious one, of course, is the Stomach Protruding into the Next Room Syndrome.

Some more subtle signs to watch for:

- MISSED MENSTRUAL PERIOD. If you have missed six periods in a row and your belly resembles a watermelon fed with Miracle-Gro, there's a good chance you may be With Child. However, you might want to consult a good lawn and garden center to be sure.

- NAUSEA. The urge to toss your cookies is, in and of itself, not a reliable indication of pregnancy. It may simply mean that you are a terrible cook or have recently quenched your thirst in a Third World country whose water purification system involves prayer to the waning moon.

    True Pregnal Nausea is marked by its suddenness and unpredictability. It will have absolutely nothing to do with anything. You will wake up, look at the dresser drawer knobs, and your stomach will react by emptying itself onto the nearest unwashable fabric.

- A FEELING OF FULLNESS. Many women find that they feel stuffed, full, uncomfortable. If you feel that way, before running off to the obstetrician, first ask yourself, Have I recently been ejected from an all-you-can-eat buffet? Is my grocery bill over $300 a week?

    If the answer is no, congratulations! You're probably pregnant, and this is simply nature's way of getting you accustomed to the sensation of having just swallowed a ten-pound leg of lamb. Whole.

- TENDER BREASTS. By nature, all breasts are on the tender side, being more delicate than, say, elbows. So when doctors ask if your breasts are tender, what they really mean is more tender than *usual*. For example, does a stiff breeze cause you discomfort? Is the bedsheet an instrument of torture? If this tenderness is accompanied by tingling ("Hey, my boobs fell asleep!"), you may indeed be pregnant.

  This is not a foolproof gauge, however. There are many other possible reasons for tingling, tender breasts, such as jogging nude in a hailstorm. Tender breasts can also be the result of common, everyday activities like braless horseback riding and slam-dancing. Also, you might want to disregard this symptom if you are, by profession, a hockey goalie.

- EXPECTANT MOTHER "GLOW." It is said that pregnant women exude a sort of "glow" that other women can spot as early as the first week after conception. This comes from hormonal changes and serves to alert people around you that you are now ravenous and will grab food off their plates if they aren't careful.

  However, you may be glowing for non-pregnancy-related reasons. Have you just had a makeover by a new, overenthusiastic Mary Kay rep? Do you do volunteer work at a nuclear power plant?

- EXTREME FATIGUE. Are you exhausted, unable to stay awake and keep up your daily responsibilities? Many women feel this way, and a good number of them turn out to be pregnant. Many of the others, however, are tired not because of a current pregnancy, but because of several previous ones. If you already have children, fatigue is not a reliable indicator. In many cases, being tired can be the result of other people's pregnancies—notably, pregnancies producing offspring such as your boss, your co-workers, your husband, etc.

- FREQUENCY OF URINATION. The urge to go to the bathroom all the time could signify nothing more than the fact that you drink way too many liquids. If you are raking in over $200 weekly on your recyclable soda cans, it's possible that this could be your problem.

MAKING IT OFFICIAL

Even with all these symptoms you'll need further corroboration of your pregnancy. It is, after all, not an Official Pregnancy until you've had Official Tests. Science, you see, is the final arbiter of who may be deemed a Genuine Preggo. Your opinion on the matter is irrelevant, and until your pregnancy can be verified by trained professionals in a laboratory, you are just another uninformed layperson with tender, tingling breasts going around making scientific claims.

Your first step will be to get a home pregnancy test. Because these tests involve private substances, such as your urine, they are done in the privacy of your own home.

First, you lock yourself in the bathroom. Then, like a deranged chemistry professor bustling about the lab in a bathrobe, you fool around the sink and toilet for a while with cups and beakers and dipsticks, feeling oddly furtive, as if you were making a bomb for the Hezbollah.

Actually, the process is not much different from high school chemistry class experiments. Except now there's a sense of meaning and urgency you found lacking while attempting to determine the pH of apple juice.

And you wait.

And wait.

You use this time to rearrange your cosmetics, practice your smile in the mirror, and wipe toothpaste splatters off the faucet, all the while keeping one eye on that test. Seconds drag into minutes, and you realize that if a watched pot never boils, the same principle may well apply to watched pee.

You check the clock. Ninety seconds have passed. By your estimation, six hours have clearly elapsed. There's something wrong with the test. Something wrong with you. You've stepped through a hole in the universe into another plane, where time stands still. At any moment H. G. Wells and Rod Serling are going to start pounding on the door, demanding to know what the hell you're doing in there.

Finally, *finally*, you see the strip change color. What a magnificent shade of blue! You should, of course, keep the strip as a memento. In fact, why not just march right down to the Sherwin-Williams color match paint chip display for a whole handful of look-alikes to hand out to your friends?

Naturally, the doctor will want to perform an Official Test to verify your results. It will, of course, be the same test, but it will be performed by people in lab coats, which automatically makes them more competent than people in terry cloth bathrobes. The obstetrician's first available appointment to do this, however, will roughly coincide with your child's first birthday.

BREAKING THE NEWS

Your next order of business will be to share the good news. If you think this will be great fun, you may be a tad disappointed. On average, nine out of ten otherwise normal, polite people, when informed of a pregnancy, will exhibit the same polished good manners and restrained curiosity shown by audiences at a taping of the "Ricki Lake Show."

You were expecting warm smiles, squeals of delight, and hearty congratulations? Not so fast there. Other than the few obvious ones who will genuinely share your joy, the only people who will be unconditionally thrilled are diaper service salespeople and the man in the next office who wants your job.

Most people eventually become overjoyed and get obsessed with your pregnancy to the point where you want to grab them by the lapels and scream, "LEAVE ME ALONE!" But their initial reaction will require some forebearance on your part.

They will behave as if this pregnancy must first meet their approval before it can be considered legitimate. Expect to be grilled and quizzed on your motives and intent, after which judgment will be passed on the wisdom and timing of this pregnancy in the guise of well-meaning comments:

"Oh! I see. Well, if that's really what you want. . . ."

"YOU?? A mother? My goodness . . . I'll have to get used to THAT picture."

"How did this happen?!"

Commentary will ensue. It will, however, always be phrased as questions to mask the fact that it is really opinion.

"Isn't it a little early to be thinking about having children?"

"Aren't you a little old for this?"

"Didn't you say you wanted to build your career first?"

"But what about your successful career?"

If you already have a child, you will be informed that the age difference is too much or too little or reminded about the added strain on your already tight budget and hectic schedule.

Be prepared with your own snappy comebacks:

Were you trying to have a baby?
A *baby*? Actually, we were trying for a Labrador retriever!

Is this something you planned?
Heavens, no. We're far too busy for that sort of

thing. We hired Planned Parenthood to handle the details.

Isn't it dangerous to have a baby at your age?
You're right. I will wait until I'm younger.

How will you ever manage with another child?
I know that with good friends like you who help out and baby-sit whenever I ask, things will work out just fine.

Do you think it's wise to bring another person into this already overpopulated world?
Beats the hell out of keeping it inside of me for the rest of my life.

Note: To those who have to deal with the "aren't you a little old for this" comments, remember Elizabeth, who scripture informs us was over eighty when she first conceived. Women at the well gave her a *very* hard time. ("Do you know how much energy it takes to bring up a prophet? You'll be ninety when John the Baptist hits school age! You'll be the only room mother with cataracts and urinary incontinence!")

TELLING DADDY

For centuries, women used to signal to their mates that they were pregnant by adopting a serene smile and knitting booties. If you were to try that today, however, the average male would assume you were making head covers for his golf clubs.

So you'll have to be a little less subtle when telling your husband. But you can still be creative. Make it memorable. Make it an adventure! Don't just blurt it out at the dinner table. ("I'm pregnant. Pass the Parmesan.") And don't call him up and leave a message with his secretary. It doesn't translate well to those pink message slips. ("WHILE YOU WERE AWAY: your wife got pregnant.")

Drop not-so-subtle hints.

- When he's away for the weekend, redecorate the gun room with Disney Babies wallpaper.
- Serve a candlelight dinner of baby peas, baby carrots, and baby back ribs in little divided plastic dishes. Complement with Dad's Root Beer. (Don't forget the bibs!) Call him Daddy.
- Throw up on him.

Should the news be coming as a particular surprise, you might not want to spring it on him while he's working with sharp tools or tweezing his nose hairs.

A WORD TO THE WISE

Some people (notably mothers and mothers-in-law) will display a certain pique at having been left out of the planning process. "Oh, my, you two are just full of surprises, aren't you?" she will say with a tight smile while buffing an imaginary scratch on the table. After she gathers herself she will cheerily announce how LOVELY it will be to have a grandchild named after someone on her side of the family—preferably her.

Note: If you have the slightest notion of what is good for you, neither your mother nor your mother-in-law must be able to claim that she was told first. Such ammunition will become a nuclear warhead in the inevitable cold war called "Who's the Favorite Grandma?" So, for your own sanity, make every attempt to deliver the news to both simultaneously. If necessary, call them from side-by-side payphones.

2
Choosing an Obstetrician/ Birth Attendant

When searching for that special someone who will have his or her hands and face between your legs on a regular basis, it's important to look for someone with whom you can build rapport.

Ideally this person should (a) speak the same language in which you normally converse and (b) not have garlic breath.

Other minimal qualifications include:

- ability to keep a straight face
- good hand-eye coordination
- short, well-manicured fingernails

It's also good if this person has some sort of educational background in pregnancy and childbirth, such as you might obtain at one of your major medical schools. Correspondence courses advertised on late-night TV are not adequate training, despite the compelling surface similarities between diesel-engine repair and episiotomies.

But do not be fooled! Having a diploma and being board-certified does not mean one knows what one is doing. Practical, hands-on experience is important too. Ask them how many episodes they've seen of "Rescue 911." Have they ever worked as a farmhand? Would they know what to do if a ham were lodged in the toilet during a blizzard?

LOOKS CAN BE DECEIVING, BUT THEY SHOULDN'T BE ALARMING

While competence, training, personality, and judgment are all good things to keep in mind, don't overlook physical appearance. Looks are considered a shallow criterion for choosing friends, but then few friendships have their basis in conversations that occur while lying on your back, peering over your belly at a face hovering in the V of your thighs.

Remember, the birth attendant will be the very first person your new baby sees when it enters the world. This is why so many babies' first order of business is to scream. So, as a kindness to the child, consider the possible effects of this obstetrician's face on an impressionable newborn.

Too, there's your own comfort to be considered. Remember, you're likely to be nauseated through much of your pregnancy anyway, and you will not want to aggravate your already hair-trigger stomach with an obstetrician whose appearance induces the same reaction as raw egg whites.

And finally, your birth attendant's appearance should not remind you of anyone in particular, because the resemblance might interfere with the doctor-patient relationship. For example, if the doctor reminds you of your ex-husband, you may feel reluctant to let him see the baby except on every other weekend.

So, you will want this person to look

- human
- reasonably sane
- attentive to normal standards of hygiene
- unlike anyone you know personally

You will *not* want this person to look like

- your ex-husband's wife
- Mike Tyson
- your boss
- the gym teacher who humiliated you in ninth grade by "accidentally" announcing over the PA system that you'd begun your period
- Dr. Kevorkian

AUDITIONING THEM FOR THE PART

Most experts suggest interviewing potential candidates to establish compatibility before selecting the one to whom you will entrust your care. As you can imagine, doctors are thrilled with this idea and will schedule time for this little chat just as soon as they can clear their calendars . . . which will coincide, roughly, with hell freezing over.

If you do manage to line up an interview, you will want to be armed with questions, which you will be able to find in any standard pregnancy preparation book. However, most doctors are on to this. They've read those very same books and memorized all the right answers.

So when you ask how the doctor feels about family involvement, he will say something soothing and enlightened-sounding, like "History has given the extended family an honored place in the miracle of birth. I heartily encourage this supporting role." What he doesn't actually say, of course, is that his idea of a supporting role is remarkably like that played by Norm's wife, Vera, on "Cheers."

Consequently, you'll have to come up with new, sneaky questions to get an accurate picture of this person's mind-set.

BE SURE TO ASK . . .

- "How do you feel about my friends filming a documentary for the junior college, chronicling my entire pregnancy, including all prenatal office visits as well as the birth?"
- "When a woman in labor screams 'SOMEBODY SHOOT ME!!'—do you do it?"
- "What percentage of your patients have to undergo psychotherapy after their birth experience?"
- "What do you consider an acceptable weight gain for an expectant mother, and are you willing to shut up about it?"

- "At Thanksgiving time, who in your family heads up the turkey cavity cleaning expedition? On average, do the giblets come out in one piece?"

MORE PREEMPLOYMENT SCREENING

If you're satisfied with the answers, you may continue your preemployment screening. Remember to be cordial and professional. Always shake hands! (This will also give you a preview of the pelvic exam. Ice-cold hands with huge, gnarled knuckles are counterindications.)

Here are a few handy suggestions for additional screening:

- Locate the prospective physician or birth attendant's high school yearbook. Check the nickname under the picture. "The Mad Professor" or "Dirtball" is not promising. Take a pass if this person was voted "Most Likely to Burn Down a Day-Care Center."
- If the physician is a male, ask him if he was ever stood up on a date. How many times? The answer can give you critical insight into his attitude toward women and the probable length of your wait for each office appointment.
- Observe the office. If the waiting room is filled with elderly men on walkers, obstetrics may be a sideline. Look for waiting rooms filled with apple-cheeked women with large bellies. (Caution: This is not foolproof. You may have simply wandered into

Milwaukee.) Check out the posters on the office walls. Leave immediately if you see one proclaiming "NO PAIN, NO GAIN."

- Inquire as to any pets this person may have. If they have names like Harlot or Slut, move on.

THE COMPATIBILITY SURVEY

If the prospective candidate has passed all of the preceding screening, you may now go on to the final stage of selection, called the *Compatibility Survey.* This operates like a computer dating service quiz inasmuch as you will be attempting to screen out people with Undesirable Qualities (such as felony convictions and stupidity) while zeroing in on persons with Desirable Qualities (such as those you would use to describe yourself).

Note: This survey is a new concept in the childbirthing arena that may be unfamiliar to the potential obstetrician, seeing as how it is just now being formulated as we speak by the author, who has not yet had a chance to enact it into law. Consequently, you might meet some resistance. Overcome this by waving your insurance card under the doctor's nose. The scent has enormously persuasive properties.

Give the candidate a number-two pencil with instructions to complete the survey quickly, completely, and honestly. Assure this person that there are no right or wrong answers, only insights into personality. Smile sweetly.

PART I

Which book title best describes you?
a. *Diary of a Madman*
b. *I'm Dysfunctional, You're Dysfunctional*
c. *I'm Good Enough, I'm Smart Enough, and Doggone It, People Like Me*

My proudest achievement in life is
a. beating that tax-evasion rap in '92
b. controlling my antifemale neurosis
c. the Nobel Prize for humanitarianism

My favorite movie is
a. *Rosemary's Baby*
b. *Misery*
c. *Birth of a Nation*

A woman's place is
a. in the stirrups
b. in the kitchen
c. behind the wheel of a shiny new Ferrari

PART II

Mark the statement that most closely mirrors your attitude.
a. Pregnant women are gross and hideous.
b. Pregnant women are beautiful.
c. All pregnant women look exactly like Demi Moore.

a. Weight gain should be limited to twenty pounds.
b. Weight gain depends on the individual.
c. Häagen-Dazs French Vanilla is an important source of calcium.

a. During childbirth, a woman should have no drugs or painkillers whatsoever.
b. A woman should be allowed mild sedatives such as NyQuil in the event of a cesarean.
c. A woman should be allowed drugs and painkillers whenever she feels like it throughout the entire process, including conception.

a. Patients are to be seen and not heard.
b. The mother's input is given the same careful consideration as financial advice from the Psychic Friends Network.
c. Your wish is my command.

SCORING

Score one point for each A, two points for each B, and three points for each C.

Candidates scoring 8-15 points either have a great sense of humor (what a kidder!) or should be approached with extreme caution such as you might use when encountering war criminals who wish to try out their new Sears Craftsman drill bit. (If you belong to an HMO with a name like Bare Minimum, don't bank on the humor angle.)

16-23 points: An acceptable, if not thrilling score. Candidates in this category seem to be trying, but all in all, you may have better luck with a kindly veterinarian.

24 points: Bingo! You have found the perfect person to deliver your baby! Unfortunately, this person is booked until the year 2020 and charges $6,000 per visit.

It should be remembered, however, that it won't matter how carefully you've selected your physician or birth attendant, because it is a Law of Nature that your baby will come when this person is on vacation or at a medical seminar entitled "Building Patient Loyalty Through Consistency of Care."

The actual labor and delivery will take place under the watchful eye of Someone Else, called "An Associate." The Associate will be someone with cold hands, gnarled knuckles, garlic breath, and two rottweilers named Slut and Harlot. Associates are always available at a moment's notice because, not having patients of their own, they do not go on vacation.

If, however, your obstetrician screws up and somehow manages to be in town when you go into labor, nature will rectify this oversight and cause you to give birth in the back of a taxicab.

3
A History of Modern Childbirth Methods

Origins of the Specious

From the beginning of time until the twentieth century, women were forced to give birth without benefit of—are you ready for this?—Popular Childbirth Theories from Every Tom, Dick, and Harry. (As if the absence of electricity, running water, and call waiting were not hardship enough.)

Throughout history, childbirth was chaotic and disorganized, with women dropping babies willy-nilly into rice paddies, soybean fields, mangers—whatever was handy. Ignorance was rampant. Women would excuse themselves from the dinner table with stomach cramps, only to return with a squalling child. ("I found it in the bathroom. Can I keep it?")

Up until the 1800s an all-female rule governed attendance at childbirth. Men were not allowed to observe, much less actually preside over, labor and delivery. Most men were more than happy to comply with this rule and, since golf or ESPN had not yet been invented, would eagerly volunteer to run off to the nearest war or invasion.

Every now and then a man would disguise himself as a woman and sneak into the birthing room, after which he would scurry back to the pub and report his findings to the incredulous townsmen. ("No way! That's impossible!")

This protocol remained until Victorian times, when male doctors, becoming bored with the daily grind of routine leechings, sought to expand their practices and declared childbirth frightening and perilous. Births at that time were, in fact, difficult and dangerous due to the incredible amount of complicated, tortuous clothing involved. The mortality rate skyrocketed as midwives by the score died horrible deaths, garroted on petticoat hoops or suffocated in mountains of crinoline.

So men charged in to save the day. ("Step aside, little lady. *I'll* handle this!") Having no idea what childbirth involved, since their medical practices had been pretty much restricted to lancing boils and trimming sideburns, doctors improvised. Looking around the shed, they gathered up whatever equipment looked vaguely obstetrical—grappling hooks, chains, fireplace tongs—and hung out their shingles.

Then came Modern Enlightenment, which coincided roughly with the discovery of revolving credit and the knowledge that there was money to be made in this birthing business. Entrepreneurs successfully set about convincing women that childbirth was a perilous undertaking requiring highly specialized skills that should be left to the experts. ("Do not try this at home!")

Home birth gave way to hospital birth. Women were happy to go along with this, not because they thought it was necessary but because it got them out of the house, where they could get some rest. Well into the sixties, women remained hospitalized for at least a week for that very reason. This continued until the midseventies, when insurance company audits determined that it was healthier for mothers to go home in a day or two.

At the same time came increased competition within the baby-birthing business. Ever more appealing marketing techniques emerged—the most popular one being the Drugged-Out-of-Your-Skull-Don't-Remember-a-Thing promotion. This could explain the baby boom of the forties and fifties. ("Hey, that wasn't so bad! Maybe I'll have nine or ten more.")

However, the effects of these drugs on the babies were not fully realized until later when signs of damage done by narcotics crossing the placental barrier began to appear in adulthood. (Television coverage of these tragic effects can be seen daily on C-SPAN.)

Consequently, trends had to be reversed. A competition ensued to see who could come up with the best method for childbirth without drugs. To keep it sporting, the competition was open only to men. Following are a few of the more interesting contenders and their methods.

READ METHOD
("CHILDBIRTH WITHOUT FEAR")

This philosophy was developed by British obstetrician Dr. Grantly Dick-Read, whose own anatomical parts gave him little to fear from the pain of childbirth.

(In fairness, however, it should be noted that Grantly Dick-Read was no stranger to pain, having endured a childhood of cruel taunting because of his dippy name.)

Dr. Dick-Read's ideas appear to stem from something he vaguely remembered from a radio address by Franklin Delano Roosevelt, who, according to historians, never actually gave birth to a child himself either. While struggling over a paper he was writing for an obscure medical journal, Grantly Dick-Read remembered Roosevelt's pronouncement that "The only thing we have to fear is fear itself." Thinking it was kind of catchy, he included it in his paper on childbirth.

Upon reading the paper, Dick-Read's colleagues stroked their beards and scowled and harrumphed and nodded so as to appear scholarly, that being the fashion of obstetric scholars at the time. "Yes, that sounds about right," they said. "Childbirth without fear. Sounds good to me. Run with it, Grantly Dick-Read. Ha-ha! What a dippy name!"

Encouraged by this response, Dr. Dick-Read formulated his theory that childbirth pain comes from fear, which causes tension, which causes pain, which causes more fear, which causes more tension, which causes more pain. Therefore, Dick-Read shrugged, women merely need to stop being afraid.

So he traveled about, spreading his message for painless childbirth. One by one, frightened pregnant women would timidly enter his office. "Don't be afraid," he said. "That'll be thirty-five dollars."

"That's it?" the women would ask. "Just 'don't be afraid'?"

"Yup. That's it. If you're afraid, you'll be tense, and then you'll have pain. And it will be *your fault.*"

His message struck a chord in women around the world, whose response could be heard ringing in unison throughout the globe: "Suck an egg, Dick-Read!"

Dick-Read knew his plan needed more work. He decided that he would dispel pain and fear through *education.* He postulated that since we most dread the unknown, why, if only women knew what to expect, they wouldn't be frightened.

So the lunatic told women what to expect.

"Look," he said comfortingly, "just imagine a small pet—a wolverine, for example—clawing its way out of your body through an opening approximately the size of a curtain ring. Is that so scary?"

Being a perceptive sort, Grantly Dick-Read sensed from the number of patients flinging themselves from his window that his technique needed refining. Still convinced that education was the key, he altered his plan slightly. He would continue telling pregnant mothers what to expect. Except now he would lie through his teeth.

"Contractions are sort of like menstrual cramps," he told them. "Many women nap or do crossword puzzles or catch up on correspondence."

Predictably, women responded much more positively to this approach. And although Dr. Dick-Read was forced to maintain an unpublished number and unlisted address for the remainder of his life, hospitals today still widely employ his method.

LAMAZE ("PAINLESS CHILDBIRTH")

One of the most popular approaches to natural childbirth is the Lamaze method, named after Frenchman Dr. Fernand Lamaze—not to be confused with Fernando Lamas, who is not French and knows nothing about childbirth except the conception part but nevertheless frequently wears a white jacket. (Both Lamaze and Lamas do, however, seem to live on their own little Fantasy Islands.)

Dr. Lamaze—who has personally never expelled anything from his own body larger than a Baby Ruth—contends that childbirth is a painless affair when done in the Proper Manner.

The Proper Manner, according to Dr. Lamaze's observations, includes *remembering to breathe.* Childbirth, you see, is an extremely distracting activity, and it is easy to overlook such minor details amid all the excitement.

The scientific terminology Lamaze gave to his technique is *psychoprophylaxis*, which derives from the Greek, meaning "Alfred Hitchcock's condoms." Lamaze admits the term has little to do with breathing and childbirth but argues that he's a fan of the great director, who, after all, did work with screaming women from time to time.

Lamaze's crusade got its start one sunny day back in the 1950s during a stroll near a maternity hospital. The shrieks emanating from the building (which sounded oddly like Janet Leigh in the shower) greatly upset the young Fernand. Understandably outraged that men should have to put up with such rude intrusions on their peaceful solitude, he vowed to do something about this whole annoying birthing business.

Lamaze puzzled over a solution until he hit on the idea of locating a country known for its compassionate leaders and state-of-the-art medical system. Naturally, the Soviet Union was the first place that came to mind.

Buoyed by heartwarming tales of Stalin and Rasputin, he traveled to Leningrad, where he observed women giving birth painlessly, as required by the Ministry of Health.

"See, this woman is not having pain," said the soldier as Dr. Lamaze peered down at the woman writhing on the bed.

Lamaze was skeptical. "Then she is possessed," he observed.

"Nyet!" barked the soldier. "She is breathing the way she is required to for glorious painless childbirth."

"AAAAAAARRRRRRRRUUUUUNNNNNN-NGHHHHHH!!" said the woman.

"That is how we breathe in Russia," explained

the soldier, hustling Lamaze quickly down the hall to see the new threshing machines.

Impressed by this, and by the Soviets' 92 percent success rate in enforcing painless childbirth, Lamaze set out to learn more at Moscow's Pavlov Institute. (THIS IS ABSOLUTELY TRUE! If you don't believe it, look it up.)

This Pavlov outfit, you will recall, is best remembered for its experiments in conditioning dogs to salivate whenever they heard a bell. Evidently, watching dogs drool rang a bell with Lamaze, and he decided women should pant during labor.

(This requires some reeducation, since most women associate panting with activities surrounding the conception part of pregnancy rather than the delivery portion.)

The upshot of all this is that the woman giving birth is not only responsible for carrying the baby and then getting it out of her body; she is also personally responsible for getting it out *properly* (translation: with the same pain-free ease of spitting watermelon seeds). Pain is a signal she's doing it *wrong*. (And frankly, if you're doing it *wrong*, honey, well, no wonder it hurts.)

Unfortunately, the Soviets fared better with the enforcement of proper breathing. So far, statisticians have located only seven people outside Russia who apparently did it the way they were supposed to. Let's chat with one.

Q: *We understand that you adhered faithfully to the breathing exercises and experienced* absolutely no pain whatsoever *during childbirth. Is this true?*

A: Yes, it is. Piece of cake. No problemo. Easy breezy. In fact, during labor, I crocheted an afghan and did my nails.

Q: *That's amazing! Quite a testimony to Dr. Lamaze's theory. Tell us, what was the most difficult part for you?*

A: Well, I'd do the deep inhale-exhale thing, and then the, you know, panting stuff, and I got a little light-headed. So I had to switch to menthol filters.

Q: *You were* smoking cigarettes *while you gave birth to your baby?!*

A: (surprised) Me? Give birth? Hell, no. I'm just here waiting for my sister to have *her* baby—that's her screaming in the next room. And who's this guy Lamaze?

LEBOYER METHOD
("CHILDBIRTH WITHOUT VIOLENCE")

Not to be outdone by Lamaze or Dick-Read, Frederick LeBoyer (who is no relation to Charles Boyer but is believed to be a distant cousin of Chef Boyardee) came up with *his* theory of childbirth. (Note, once again, the male gender here. Do you see a pattern?)

LeBoyer, appalled by what he saw of childbirth in movies such as *Alien* and *The Fly*, decided that this whole birthing business was far too violent and should be conducted in a more civilized manner. If childbirth itself is violent, his logic went, babies will grow up to be violent themselves. Recent congressional hearings about violence on television echo this theory, and legislation is now being drafted to levy huge fines or even imprisonment against any woman in labor watching "Beavis and Butthead" or any televised hockey game during the last stages of childbirth.

According to Chef Boyardee's cousin, the baby should not be forced out into the world; it should be *coaxed*. Presumably this can be accomplished through the use of various bribes waved about at the entrance to the birth canal. ("Lookee what the nice doctor has for da wittle baby! Ooooh, SpaghettiOs!")

Instead of barking commands at the mother to *push*, obstetricians should evidently murmur, "Nudge." Unfortunately, the nonviolent atmosphere is, at this juncture, pretty unilateral. So far, no one has figured out how to get the infant to go along with the program. All efforts have failed to persuade baby that it's not *nice* to use its head as a battering ram on mommy for sixteen hours.

LeBoyer's method also calls for a peaceful atmosphere in the delivery room. This means turning out all the lights and putting the baby immediately on the mother's tummy so that they can "bond." LeBoyer's disciples are, however, still working on a couple of teensy glitches that can occur in the dark when no one can see anything—such as the baby falling to the floor and the mother later finding out that she has bonded with the placenta.

Since loud noise also is considered Violence against the baby, LeBoyer's theory necessitates excluding some of the noisiest and most distressing sounds of the delivery room. Unfortunately, that usually means the mother.

Another feature of Leboyer's method is a warm

bath following birth, a reassuring gesture to return baby to the familiar sensation of being suspended in amniotic fluid. Most people think a bath is a good idea anyway, considering the untidy state in which most babies emerge.

This also makes the babies much more photogenic for their first picture and eliminates tactless observations such as "Oh, my. He looks just like a veal parmigiana."

OTHER, LESSER-KNOWN CHILDBIRTH METHODS

Medical science is continually making strides to come up with new, weirder ways to make the birth process memorable.

ROY ROGERS METHOD

Mother assumes the traditional in-the-stirrups position and has a saddle block. The baby is then lassoed with the umbilical cord.

LAWNMOWER MAN VIRTUAL REALITY BIRTHING

The father of the child puts on special headgear and, strapped to a John Deere riding mower, cuts the grass while simultaneously giving birth.

RUSH LIMBAUGH METHOD

Used when the enormous size of the head would be too painful to tolerate. Everyone is totally anesthetized.

QUEER NATION METHOD

The mother hides in the closet, and the baby is outed *for* her whether she's ready or not.

AFL-CIO ORGANIZED LABOR

Labor lasts eight hours max, with frequent breaks. Any overtime must be negotiated through collective bargaining.

POPPIN' FRESH METHOD

Busy mothers' time-saver. Family members merely grasp Mom by the ankles and whack her against the countertop—out pops baby!

SUSAN POWTER'S
STOP THE INSANITY METHOD

Instead of shaving the mother's pubic region, hospital personnel shave her head.

CONGRESSIONAL HEARINGS METHOD

Mother listens to Senate Banking Committee testimony and immediately becomes numb from the ears down. When asked about her experience, she will repeat over and over, "I have no recollection of that."

4

Physical Changes

Body by Boeing

Get used to the idea of expansion. Because, naturally, if you're going to have a person living inside of you—lolling around, eating all day, calling your uterus home—you'll need to make some adjustments for its living space. In other words, you'll have to get as big as a house.

Psychologically, you're going to have to ease into this. Think Barbie's Dream House.

In a culture where the Barbie doll has defined the ideal for the female form, pregnancy comes as quite a shock to the old body image. Someone with a calculator and insufficient workplace supervision once figured out that Barbie's measurements, scaled to life size, translated to 40-18-32. One day Mattel is going to run out of perky Barbie themes and put out Third Trimester Barbie, whose measurements will be a lifelike 40-81-40 (varicose veins sold separately).

HOW BIG IS BIG?

Body types, of course, differ, and what changes your body undergoes will necessarily depend on what you started out with. To get an idea of what you will look like as a fully pregnant person, find your body type and its correlating comparisons in this before-and-after chart.

Before:	Demi Moore
After:	Danny DeVito
Before:	Bette Midler
After:	Orson Welles
Before:	Roseanne
After:	Oliver Hardy
Before:	Sally Struthers, 1971
After:	Sally Struthers, 1995
Before:	Goldie Hawn
After:	Delta Burke

BIG CHANGES IN
THE PARTS DEPARTMENT

But there's much, much more to pregnancy than just getting big. If being enormous were the only prerequisite for having a baby, all calls to Planned Parenthood would have been long ago routed to Richard Simmons.

But no, an authentic working pregnancy requires that your body undergo a whole host of other delightful changes. Nothing will remain the same, inside or out. Your body will be in a constant state of turmoil, due to the necessary rearrangement of your interior furnishings to make room for baby in impossibly cramped quarters. Mother Nature will handle the design logistics ("OK, I want her kidneys over *here*, and the bladder goes *there* . . .").

There are roughly 17,402 changes your body must go through before you can deliver your baby. DO NOT SKIP ANY OF THEM! Each physical manifestation of pregnancy is like an ingredient or preparation instruction in a recipe. Before you leave out anything, consider that the only difference between steak tartare and beef jerky is smoke.

Here are a few of the non-negotiables:

BOOBS, GLORIOUS BOOBS!

One of the first signs of pregnancy is enlargement of the breasts. At first you might think this is great fun, particularly if, up until now, your shoulder blades have provided your only cleavage. Your husband will think this is for his benefit and will behave as if he were a small boy with a new pony.

You'll throw Boob Bashes, little celebratory fetes in honor of your new dimensions. And, oh, those candlelight dinners! You'll be a gourmet delight, serving up breasts-on-the-half-shell for his dining pleasure in your newly purchased Frederick's of Hollywood "Obscene Cuisine" demi-bra.

For a few glorious weeks, you're in hooter heaven. BUT . . .

Look Out, She's Gonna Blow!

. . . this enlargement continues, rapidly escalating to startling proportions such as found among women with names like Tempest Bazongas.

You may be approached on the street by smarmy lawyers who want to represent you in implant liability lawsuits. Your blouses and suits will gap between the buttonholes, creating tempting pockets into which co-workers will slide pencils and then collapse on the floor in hysterics.

And still they keep growing. Larger, larger, like prize-winning 4-H project cantaloupes. Wandering through the state fair horticulture building, someone pins a blue ribbon on you.

Unaccustomed to your new dimensions, you miscalculate clearance distances. (Remember the stove scene in *Mrs. Doubtfire?*) You knock over your water glass when reaching for the pepper and drag yourself through the fettuccine. Squeezing past pedestrians and seated restaurant patrons becomes an adventure. ("Excuse me, madam, could you remove your breast from my ear?")

In the car you honk the horn or change the radio station every time you inhale. A sneeze while you're in the elevator means a stop at every floor. Turn suddenly, and some poor child gets a knockout breast to the jaw.

And now they *hurt*. You roll over in bed and dream you're having a mammogram. The shower is an instrument of torture. ("*Who* filled the shower head with straight pins?") You avoid revolving doors and crowded malls, knowing that the slightest bump could send you into orbit.

Deep down you know that you could, at any moment, explode—raining boob shrapnel over a six-block radius.

And then there's the matter of what to *do* with them. There is just simply nowhere to *put* them anymore. You can't just unstrap your breasts at the end of the day and prop them in the corner like scuba tanks. Where you go, they go. It's like some joker thought it would be funny to Super Glue two five-pound flour sacks to your chest.

Sitting in a restaurant booth, you have two options. You can sit way back, employing great skill and precision to negotiate the vast distance over which your fork must travel to transfer the food from the plate to your mouth. If you are skilled in robotics or arcade games involving cranes and stuffed animals, this could work.

Your other option is to scoot up close and lay your breasts on the table. (Etiquette books only mention keeping your *elbows* off the table. They are silent on the matter of breasts.) It is, however, considered good manners to make sure your companion has taken up his silverware first, and certainly you should avoid plopping them down on his butter plate.

Bedtime, however, is the worst. You consider digging a trench in the mattress so you can lie on your stomach. If you get too close to the edge of the bed, one of them will hurl itself over the side and take you with it like an anchor.

What Will I Look Like?

To get an idea of what you can expect in the boob department, try this simple little experiment: Take four balloons—two pink (representing the nonpregnant boobs) and two multicolored swirl ones (representing the pregnant boobs). Fill the pink ones with helium, the two swirly ones with water.

See the difference?

Now, for a sneak preview of a nine-month boob, add more water to one of the swirly balloons. Stand at the faucet (use this time to catch up on your reading) until the balloon resembles satellite pictures of Jupiter.

Note: It is important that you use the swirl-design balloons, because they accurately simulate the surprising array of colorful veins and capillaries that will show up to decorate your breasts.

You should not consider these veins and capillaries disfiguring. In fact, welcome them! They are nature's own protective coloration for your painfully tender breasts. In the wild, Mother Nature uses bright colors to warn off predators from a particularly tasty-looking morsel. Similarly, a pregnant woman now bears her own protective coloration, giving her mate the same warning issued by poisonous butterflies and snakes—*TOUCH THEM AND YOU DIE.*

The Bigger They Are, the Harder They Fall

Of course, all this is temporary. You need not fear a lifetime of looking like you're hauling muskmelons to market. Your breasts will return to Normal after your pregnancy. But before you get too excited, you should know the word *normal*, when used in this context, refers to Normal, Illinois, whose city limits—when outlined on a map—roughly resemble a banana.

To get an idea of what your postpregnancy Normal Breast will look like, try the following:

Women who were small-breasted before pregnancy: Take a L'eggs nylon knee-high stocking and drop a golf ball into the toe.

Women who were big-breasted before pregnancy: On an overhead projector, carefully observe the state map of Florida.

There is no need to fear that, after pregnancy, your breasts will suddenly deflate and go flying about the room like a balloon with the air let out. The process is more like a slow leak caused by a pinhole—hardly noticeable to bystanders, except for that annoying high-pitched whistling sound. (Any leftover skin can be gathered with a rubber band to form a rosette and passed off as a brooch.)

THAT AMAZING EXPANDING STOMACH

You've seen pictures. You've seen actual real-life women in their third trimester. Still, it's hard to comprehend that it can—and is—happening to you.

You imagine looking like a serene madonna, cloaked in an ethereal mist like a Renaissance painting, your hands folded maternally over the round swell of your belly. (Hark, are those angel harps I hear?) There is, of course, the possibility that this will be precisely the way you will look. There is also the possibility that Snoop Doggy Dogg may one day sing at the Vatican.

Or perhaps you envision yourself looking like Demi Moore on the cover of *Vanity Fair*. Adjusting the fantasy for realism, this will play out something more along the lines of *Dudley* Moore. With a tumor.

It starts out slowly—a little tummy too adorable for words. You stroke it and pat it and admire its gentle round curve. Just a little pooch belly. Barely noticeable, especially now that your breasts are hogging all the attention.

Eventually, however, your stomach will catch up. Slowly, imperceptibly, steadily inflating as if you had pulled up to the air pump at the service station, unscrewed the cap on your navel, and put the hose in.

And as your breasts get fuller (and longer), your stomach will also be getting fuller and higher. Eventually, they will meet. Out of room and in desperate need of space, your stomach rises between your breasts, forcing them to flop to either side like basset hound ears.

And still the inflating continues. Concerned for your safety, your husband makes hourly checks with the tire gauge, pressing it against your navel. He takes the reading and shakes his head. Frowning, he informs you gravely that the all-weather radials on the pickup take only forty pounds before they blow.

After about six months, you will begin to get vaguely uncomfortable about your skin's capacity to keep stretching. By the eighth month you'll really start to panic. You see no possible way for your skin to keep up with this—it's just a matter of time before you burst like a baked potato in a microwave.

Relax! The key here is elasticity, a concept best illustrated by observing how a bubble is blown.

(In fact, it was one man's Freudian fascination with pregnancy that led to the invention of bubble gum. Millions of people every day, though they imagine they are merely chewing gum and blowing bubbles, are actually re-creating the fantasies of Bazooka Joe, who, although he was unable actually to become pregnant or give birth himself, devoted his life to paying tribute to the process. Bazooka Joe, you will recall, was the fellow who wore his turtleneck halfway up his head, as if he were perpetually emerging from the birth canal—a state of never-ending "crowning.")

At any rate, the pregnant stomach has a lot in common with well-executed bubbles. The best ones are formed very slowly, with patience and constant, even pressure so as not to burst the bubble. Done properly, you could blow a bubble large enough to house a small pet. In fact, there are machines in the mall that will do this.

These machines can give you a pretty good picture of how this stomach thing works. Go to the mall. After stopping at the Fudge Factory, Ben & Jerry's, the rest room, Mrs. Fields, the Popcorn Shoppe, and the bathroom again, locate one of those kiosks where they sell custom-made giant balloons with things in them, like teddy bears. Using a special colorless balloon placed over a machine that stretches the opening to enormous sizes, they will gently inflate the balloon

. . . slowly . . . slowly . . . bigger, bigger . . . until it's large enough for the stuffed toy.

Pregnancy works the same way, except *your* opening is stretched out much later and, unlike a balloon, has a rich blood supply and nerve endings. But the inflating part is pretty accurate. Still, it's hard to *really* comprehend with just a plush toy. For greater authenticity, try this: Smile sweetly, fork over your money, then hand the clerk a squirming piglet. ("It's an anniversary surprise for my husband.")

To further reproduce the cozy womblike environment, add water. (Bonus: An entertaining, yet effective simulation device for water-breaking rehearsals. Simply tuck under your skirt and wander about the mall. For extra fun, sit down next to an elderly couple with oxygen tanks.)

Things to Do with Your Belly Button

Eventually, your stomach grows so big that there is no more room for storing anything besides baby. One day your belly button will just *POP* out, like a turkey timer.

Unfortunately, this does not signal that the darling little Butterball is done. You could go on for weeks with your belly button protruding like an extra nose. And yes, it will poke through your clothes. Well-meaning friends will brush at it to smooth it down, thinking it's a bunch in the fabric ironed in at the cleaners.

Make use of your turkey timer. Use your imagination! Here are a few suggestions to get you started.

- Dress up a plain maternity shift for evening by hanging strands of pearls from it.
- No more shower mishaps slipping on the soap! Merely use your navel as a handy hook for Soap on a Rope.
- Never again misplace those car keys! Hung securely on your belly button, they're always right at hand.
- Arms full of packages? Ring doorbells and push elevator buttons simply and easily with a simple buck of the belly.

Stretch Marks . . . Nature's Little Tread Marks

But even the most elastic material has its limits. As happens in most cases when you stretch material that's too small over something that's too big—such as pulling a nylon footie over a rump roast—there's going to be tearing.

However, in instances when the material happens to be pregnant human flesh, the tears you observe are called *stretch marks*—reddish purple slashes on your belly such as you might find on small children left alone in a room with Magic Markers. You will try to scrub them off to no avail.

On closer inspection, you will realize that they are actual *gouges*, like dirt-bike wheelies on a wet lawn.

(Stretch marks don't hurt, but to the untrained eye they look as if they do. So you could, if you want, get some major mileage out of this. Lie down on the couch and moan pitifully while holding your belly. Raise your shirt and show him where it hurts. Smile

bravely and inform your husband that Godiva chocolates are reputed to offer *some* small measure of relief.
Keep a sheet of paper tucked between the cushions,
and every now and then s-l-o-w-l-y rip off a corner.
Shriek hideously.)

Actually, you won't *really* be lying about the Godiva chocolates, because Experts suggest massaging
cocoa butter into your skin to help keep the skin sup-
ple and elastic. And what, pray tell, might the active
ingredient in chocolate be? Bingo! Cocoa butter. And
since stretch marks occur beneath the skin layers,
well, it just stands to reason that internal applications could be very therapeutic.

Experts and pregnancy manuals will reassure
you that your stretch marks will eventually fade to
little silver streaks and be hardly noticeable. "Eventually," used in this context, means ten years. "Little
silver streaks," while sounding almost elegant—a bit
of glitz for the evening—will actually look as if silver-
fish have crawled up from the basement and em-
bedded themselves under your skin.

The Experts are, however, right about the hardly
noticeable part. Your stretch marks will be hidden in
the wrinkles and folds of loose excess skin, in much
the same way as pulled threads go unnoticed on
pleated crepe. For *really* unnoticeable stretch marks,
have several babies.

Which brings us to . . .

Postpartum Paunch

No one expects what happens to her body after childbirth. Perhaps if little girls grew up with a line of

Reproductive Barbies, we wouldn't have this problem. Accustomed to playing with Postpartum Barbie with its lifelike chicken flesh that can be styled and re-styled over and over again into any number of exciting fashions ("tie a big poufy bow or drape into a slouchy sash"), mothers would not be shocked at what remains after baby is born.

The first time you see your stomach after you have your baby, you will become hysterical. You will lift up your hospital gown and see it lying there in billowing folds, like a parachute descended into the treetops, draped all over you.

You will cry.

But Experts assure you that your Amazing Elastic Stomach will snap right back into shape, like a Stretch Armstrong doll or a smooshed Nerf ball. And guess what? This time the Experts are right! Sorta.

It won't spring *right* back, but after a few weeks some measure of elasticity will return. At this stage you will be able to pick up a handful and twirl it above your head like pizza dough.

But even though pizza dough can stretch to amazing diameter, way out across the pastry board, it will eventually shrink, slowly creeping back into itself at a snail's pace, regaining form, until finally it's back to the tight compact condition it started in.

Almost.

5
Discomforts, Complaints, and Aggravations

As Gilda Radner's Rosanne Rosannadanna used to say: "It's always something."

Your body will undergo all sorts of unpleasant little changes that appear to be totally unrelated to babygrowing. They are, in fact, little evolutionary glitches in the reproductive process. Cosmic hiccups.

It might seem, at first blush, that the primary purpose of these symptoms is to irritate you and cause you discomfort. Well, that's part of it. But they also serve a larger purpose; in fact, they provide real benefit.

For without them, you would not be so eager to go through labor and delivery. After nine months of suffering through a never-ending parade of pointless aches, pains, and malfunctioning body parts, you start warming up to the idea of getting it all over with in one MAJOR ordeal. ("Let me get this straight. You mean all I have to do to be normal

49

again is, for twenty-two hours, undergo the equivalent of lying in a functioning trash compactor, after which I will expel something the size of a poodle through one of my smallest orifices? Let's DO it!")

The routine assaults and indignities visited upon your poor body are also effective reminders that having a baby will forever alter both your body and your life. Think of your vast array of annoying symptoms as Nature's little Post-It Notes—memos from reality that life, as you know it, is over.

THE BIGGIES

MORNING SICKNESS

First off, *morning sickness* is a very, very misleading label. Nausea during pregnancy is no more confined to morning hours than Dawn dish detergent. It's an anytime, anywhere kind of thing. The authorities should take immediate steps to reeducate the public by declaring Vomit Awareness Week, then seizing every pregnancy book in existence and scratching out the word *morning* wherever it occurs, replacing it with *Ninety Days and Ninety Nights.*

The Experts will tell you that morning sickness is your body's normal reaction to your rapidly changing hormones. This is another deception. If this were true, upchucking would be epidemic in our nation's high schools, where berserk adolescent hormones go on a daily rampage, flying down the hallways, ricocheting off the lockers. Just think about all the heaving there'd be on the set of "Beverly Hills 90210" alone.

Besides, men have hormones, and, with the exception of college undergraduates, they don't go around ralphing all over the place.

No, what's really happening is housekeeping. Mother Nature is clearing out and cleaning out, tidying the guest quarters for your new baby. Ruthlessly, she tosses everything out. ("Just look at this mess! This has got to go. What's with all these peas? And corn . . . ! Girl, you've got corn everywhere. What *are* you keeping this stuff for?")

Knowing *why* it's happening is, however, little comfort as day after day you shout into that big porcelain telephone. You try to figure out things you can put in your stomach that Mother Nature won't throw back. Would she like a Big Mac? An egg? How about some nice Oreos with Cool Whip, huh huh huh?

No, you didn't think so.

You try everything—meat, fruit, vegetables, bread—trying to come up with the one thing that will stay down. Because, unlike *normal* nausea, such as the kind that comes with the flu or being tossed about the waves in a dinghy, pregnal nausea does not cause you to lose your appetite. You are desperately, ravenously hungry. In fact, everything sounds good, everything tastes good, but it will immediately come right back up, as if Mother Nature were down there—waiting, lurking, hiding behind your esophagus—just ready to shoot that stuff back up with her catapult.

The quest for the Perfect Food is, however, futile because there is no rhyme or reason to morning sickness. Your stomach isn't rejecting a *particular* food; it's rejecting food at random. Capriciously. Willy-nilly. Because it's raining. Because it's sunny. Because the phone's ringing. Like tax audits and customs inspections, there doesn't have to be a reason. In fact, there usually isn't.

But in your natural quest for sense and order in your life, you will try to understand the logic behind your nausea. Surely there must be a pattern! But of course there isn't. Even if you were to write everything down, faithfully recording every food, every smell, every upchuck, you would only conclude that *everything* makes you sick.

Including your husband. Because smells can really trip the old eject lever. Your husband's cologne, the same stuff that you've loved for years and makes you feel all good inside, is still going to affect your insides, but you're not gonna love it.

And just because something stays down one time doesn't mean it's going to stay down the next. ("But I could have sworn Cheez Whiz was OK!") Still, you hold out hope of finding that one elusive stomach-compatible food. In the unlikely event that this does occur, the Magic Morsel will invariably be something highly unappetizing to everyone else, such as eel, or available only in one specialty restaurant, for example Chez Tater Tots, open from noon till five on Thursdays.

The Experts' answer for all this nausea nonsense is saltine crackers. No matter what, just keep eating those dry crackers. Keep them by your bed and stuff your face with them at every opportunity. No one knows who thought this up and why (a good guess would be the CEO of Nabisco).

You will throw these up too.

VARICOSE VEINS

At some point in your pregnancy, you may look down at your legs and find that they resemble the contents of a can of pickled squid.

Relax! These are simply what's known as *varicose veins* (from the Latin, *vari*, meaning "very," and *cose*, meaning "gross"). They are a naturally occurring physiological response to the rigors of walking up and down the aisles of the baby department and standing in line for the bathroom.

Doctors suggest that you can minimize the incidence of varicose veins by keeping your legs raised above your heart. While this is exceptionally useful workplace advice if you are a Rockette, or employed as a demonstrator for Craftmatic beds, it may be somewhat more difficult for you to incorporate this posture into your daily routine. However, you can, while riding the subway, elevate your legs by using the hand straps as stirrups.

One of the contributing culprits, say the Experts, is constricting stockings, and you are cautioned to avoid them. *Then*, in the next breath, the same schizophrenic Experts tell you to rush out and get yourself some support hose to prevent varicose veins. It is evidently the manner in which the stockings are used that makes all the difference, and there should be warning labels on the packages. CAUTION: USE ONLY ACCORDING TO PACKAGE DIRECTIONS. NOT TO BE USED AS A TOURNIQUET. MISUSE OF PRODUCT CAN CAUSE LEG VEINS TO SWELL UP LIKE OVERCOOKED LINGUINE.

HEMORRHOIDS

"Your sore veins . . . you prob'ly think this chapter's about you . . ."
—*Carly Simon singing about hemorrhoids*

What differentiates these veins from varicose veins is their highly inconvenient and *painful* location—an area of the body normally reserved for activities involving toilet paper and a good book. Known among the sisterhood of sufferers by the deceptively benign code name *hanging vines*, hemorrhoids are vicious, nasty, and a literal pain in the arse.

If you get hemorrhoids, there is no way to hide the fact. The entire world knows the meaning of that telltale Tim Conway slow-shuffle walk, combined with your tortured facial grimace and one twitching eye. It is like trying to act nonchalant with a lit sparkler between your legs.

The mere act of sitting becomes a precision gymnastics routine. Mary Lou Retton's Olympic balance beam performance pales in comparison to the skill with which hemorrhoid sufferers can precariously balance the weight of their entire body on one cheek on the edge of the chair.

Hemorrhoids, unlike their more visible counterparts, varicose veins, cannot be blamed on your stockings—unless of course you're engaging in some *very* strange pantyhose-related activities, which are not recommended by the manufacturer's directions on the package.

About the only helpful advice the experts can offer on how to escape hemorrhoids is to "avoid constipation"—a bit of wisdom predicated on the unlikely notion that people routinely make deliberate efforts to become constipated and they need only be alerted to the error of their ways.

Since varicose veins are eased by keeping your legs elevated, it stands to reason that the same strategy would work for hemorrhoids. Elevating the affected area in this case is, however, somewhat more difficult to accomplish discreetly and, unless you have a private office, should not be attempted at work.

Hemorrhoid sufferers used to be given little inner tubes to sit on—"doughnuts" as they were called. As it turns out, these things made the condition worse, and women would have gotten more relief from sitting on an angel food cake. The doughnut hole, you see, merely allowed gravity to target the offending area, encouraging the hanging vines to descend and send out runners into the couch.

So it is now recommended that you use ice to reduce the swelling. If the sharp edges of ice cubes do not appeal to you, try sitting on a frozen pizza. (Keep the plastic wrap on. As it thaws, the pepperoni can be irritating to inflamed tissues.)

BACKACHE

It is not unusual to experience nagging, unrelenting backaches, as so often occurs when you carry a bowling ball on your person for weeks at a time.

Of course, in those instances relief is available and almost instantaneous when you discover the link and set the ball down. Preggos, however, cannot set the ball down until the ball's good and ready to be set down.

With their typical brilliance, Experts address your backache problem by submitting the helpful observation that you should avoid carrying anything heavy and certainly never straight out in front. While it is understandable that they may have overlooked the little fact that this is PRECISELY WHY YOU *HAVE* THE BACKACHE, it is worth keeping in mind when in the vicinity of bowling balls.

MINOR LEAGUE BUT STILL ANNOYING

GINGIVITIS

Gingivitis, as you know, is bleeding of the gums—presumably caused by not brushing your teeth after playing gin rummy. But pregnant women can get it for no good reason.

Dentists do not wish to discuss the reasons that gingivitis occurs in expectant women. They are used to dealing with only one *public* orifice of your body and will start stuffing large wads of cotton packing in your mouth and running the drill really really loud if you start talking about matters involving other orifices.

However, it is theorized that the body, accustomed to monthly menstruation and now frustrated and confused, goes haywire and reroutes the whole shebang up through your gums.

Something somewhere's gotta bleed.

EDEMA

This is a serious condition caused by fluid retention wherein your ankles and wrists transform themselves into overstuffed knockwurst. Persons with edema should keep the affected parts elevated and avoid tanning beds, since these act like commercial hot dog cookers, causing you to plump while you're cooking. The application of mustard and relish is not advised.

Your fingers will also swell up, so rings should be taken off early in pregnancy. If you do not, your fingers will look like cocktail franks tied off in the middle with fishing line. Worse, the rings act as little metal tourniquets, clamping off blood supply, with much the same results as clamping off an umbilical cord. If you do forget to take them off and the worst happens, a jar of formaldehyde can serve as your jewelry box. ("Wanna see my wedding ring?")

FREQUENT URINATION

Your fingers, ankles, and feet are the only parts of your body that will be capable of retaining water. The rest of your body will be a sieve. Not only does your bladder shrink to the size of a thimble to make room for baby; it suddenly goes completely berserk and has the attention span of a hyperactive two-year-old.

Since there's no way to administer Ritalin directly to the bladder, you will become intimately familiar with the precise location of every bathroom in a five-county area. You will chart wall maps noting every strategic location with pushpins and carry travel maps in the car. (AAA now has a special trip-planning service that provides ratings for all the rest rooms along your route. A three-star designation indicates short lines, wide stalls, and quick access without having to beg for a key that appears to unlock the castle drawbridge.)

You will plan your day around bathrooms, questioning friends thoroughly before accepting any invitation to an activity where *immediate* access is iffy. ("Picnic? Would that be in a park?") ("Just how far off shore do you plan on taking this boat? Twenty feet? Thirty?")

In desperate situations you will become more assertive than you ever dreamed possible. Long lines in the ladies' room? No problem when there's a men's room next door. You'll charge in without a second thought. There will always be at least one gentleman who'll give a lady his seat.

Since even the sound of running water can set you off, you will learn to avoid any danger zones— e.g., shopping centers with center mall fountains, restaurants with busboys refilling water pitchers.

HEARTBURN

As baby grows and tries to get comfortable in those cramped quarters, naturally it will try to push away any organs that may be crowding it, such as your stomach. There aren't too many available space options, so baby will attempt to relocate it to the nearest exit, which happens to be north. Unfortunately, your stomach contains gastric juices, which are benign substances while in the stomach but caustic elsewhere. When they escape into your esophagus, the overall effect is something like a Molotov cocktail.

Experts will tell you that this is perfectly normal. (What else is new?) It is, of course, perfectly normal, in much the same way it is perfectly normal for nail polish remover to dissolve the finish on your coffee table.

The worst thing you can do for this is to lie down. The acid will then bubble up through your nose, drip onto the bed, and eat a hole in the mattress. So you must sleep sitting up. But of course you can't do this, because you will have your feet up for the varicose veins and edema and your behind up in the air for the hemorrhoids.

CHLOASMA

This, for those of you who don't speak Greek, is the famed "mask of pregnancy," that charming skin condition that makes you look like you were sponge-painted with sunless tanning lotion.

Chloasma occurs when a small group of scattered skin pigment cells suddenly lose their minds and think they've gone to the Bahamas for a week. The rest of your cells remain sane and stay the same color.

Again, Experts blame those raging hormones. (At least they don't suggest saltine crackers.) The good news is, this will go away. But for the next few months, resign yourself to helpful friends who will wet their thumbs and rub at the smudges. ("Whaddya got braunschweiger smeared all over your face for?")

LINEA NIGRA

More Adventures in Pigmentation! One day you will wake up, look down, and find that someone has taken a laundry marker to your belly—either that, or you've been abducted by aliens and dissected aboard the mother ship with only the scar as proof for the tabloids. A dark line now runs from your pubic bone to your navel and has absolutely no purpose except as a plumb line to make sure you've got your skirt on straight.

HAIR AND NAILS

Because of those wacky hormones of yours, increased blood supply, and some dandy prenatal vitamins, your hair and nails are going to grow like crazy. Most women are delighted with this, until they realize that without continual maintenance they can easily end up looking like a crazed hermit.

And don't forget, those toenails will keep growing too! Unfortunately, after the seventh month you won't be able to reach them with the nail clippers. Eventually your toenails will slice open your shoes by day and lacerate your husband's ankles by night. But they do come in handy with the yardwork; edge the lawn with just a leisurely barefoot stroll. On the other hand, small pets should be safely secured in another room when you're walking around barefoot. You wouldn't want to explain to the children how Fluffy died.

And while you're tossing your long, luxurious tresses, take a gander under those armpits. ("Anybody seen the Weed Whacker?") Those legs could use a couple of passes with the John Deere, too. And check out that upper lip! Might want to do something about that, unless, of course, you live in a country where olive oil is considered a beverage.

6

Dressing for Excess

When you first discover that you are going to have a baby, you can't *wait* to get into those maternity clothes. You'll be itching to don the Official Uniform and adopt the Official Stance. (Feet apart, exaggerated swayback, arms resting across stomach, while strains of Paul Anka's "Havin' My Baby" play in the background.)

You will zoom off to the mall and screech to a stop in front of stores with precious names like Lady in Waiting and Great Expectations. As you flip through the racks of clothes, you will realize with mounting excitement that each item is too cute for words. Just *adorable*. Darling darling darling.

Then it hits you. Suddenly, you realize just *why* they are so darling. They are all oversized children's clothes, dipped in vats of sherbet colors, with whimsical woodland creatures romping about the lapels and bodice. Not a navy blue or charcoal in the bunch. The children's labels have all been carefully removed and replaced with ones from fake design houses such as Pregnant Paws.

AND, you realize with a shudder, *you are going to have to wear these things to work.*

Yes, for the next several months your Power Wardrobe will bear a striking resemblance to the toddler's dress department at Sears.

Evidently the Chief Fashion Designer of the World had just a few too many martinis one day and muddled the distinction between *expecting* a child and *looking* like one. (So far, clothes designers haven't seemed to notice this little error, which is understandable considering how busy they must be with *real* fashion priorities, such as locating malnourished teenagers to model evening gowns made of trout scales.)

At a time in her life that a woman most needs to feel mature, competent, and capable of handling the enormous responsibilities that go with motherhood, she is required to dress like an enormous Shirley Temple doll. (If you currently wear your hair in sausage curls, now's the time for that new do.)

On the other hand, Shirley Temple did grow up to be a U.S. ambassador, once again proving that with tenacity and the tap-dancing skills so valued in diplomatic circles, one can overcome the career disadvantages associated with ruffled underpants.

If you work in a day-care center, pediatrician's office, or Chuck E. Cheese, such clothes may even be a career asset. Customers and co-workers will think you're really into your work and your Little Girl look is intended to carry out a theme.

However, the corporate world offers less latitude. Most people—strange as it may seem—are oddly leery about engaging the services of an accountant or lawyer dressed like Heidi.

THE POWER SUIT

Unfortunately, there are only two options for the boardroom. If you don't care to conduct business while smocked, shirred, and decorated with duckies and bunnies and bows, you have but one other choice: outrageously expensive Boutiques and Shoppes—not to be confused with reasonably priced stores and shops—where the expectant businesswoman can find clothes that will make her look exactly like Winston Churchill.

These actual corporate-looking maternity business suits cost only two or three times more than a regular suit. Evidently elastic waistbands are far more costly than painstakingly tailored, hand-sewn waistbands and finely worsted wool. Of course, you must also be charged for the enormous inconvenience of *not* having to precisely tailor the suit to exacting specifications.

Unfortunately, this overpriced pinstriped maternity business suit is about your only shot at some semblance of dignity. It may, in fact, make you appear almost businesslike. Strong. Confident. Commanding. Or—more accurately—Nero Wolfe in drag.

But it is, at this juncture, your only alternative to looking like the Toddler That Ate New York.

THE HART SCHAFFNER & MARX CONSPIRACY

Men, of course, do not have to put up with such sartorial indignities. Why is this? It is a hair-pulling, teeth-gnashing paradox. Pregnant women cannot buy *real* clothes, but their male counterparts—men whose bellies approximate the third trimester with twins—can waltz into any store and instantly be fitted with actual, authentic, grown-up clothes.

Men of sizable dimension are not relegated to little strip mall shoppes with clever names like Gut Reaction or Le Lardasse.

Men's clothiers do not have a separate line of suits for potbellies. They merely have a wide range of sizes of the same style. It's not as if designers are incapable of creating normal clothes to fit people with oversized bellies or generous girth. (It is, after all, possible for Brooks Brothers to make business suits for Ted Kennedy and Dom DeLuise.)

Nor are men required to wear suit jackets with precious little appliqués and embroidery whose specific purpose is to draw attention to their "condition." Were potbellied men subject to the same fashion rules as pregnant women, they would be wearing suits with petit point pigs and Budweiser Clydesdales cavorting up and down their lapels.

It is the gestational version of the Scarlet Letter. For their carnal activities women are sentenced to parade about in maternity T-shirts emblazoned with "BABY!" and an arrow pointing down.

Men, however, are not branded for the consequences of activities involving Big Macs and Miller Genuine Draft. There are no T-shirts with arrows pointing south screaming "FAT!" or "CORONARY IN WAITING."

You could, of course, make your own clothes. Assuming you would actually know how to do such a thing, this would pose a solution except for the fact that the maternity fashion people are way ahead of you. They have rounded up the few existing patterns for grown-up maternity clothes and replaced them with the Official Preschool Maternity Patterns.

Which leads to your only option—improvising.

EVERYDAY HOUSEHOLD ITEMS YOU CAN WEAR

For the first four months you can get by with your "fat clothes"—clothes that are too big for everyday wear yet not too big to give away. Leaving the button open on the slacks with a big shirt over it adds another week or so. Shoulder pads help balance the look and deceive the eye; for appropriately sized ones, check the garage for boat cushions.

When that no longer works, you must get really creative. Here are a few tips to get you started:

• Replace hook-and-eye or frog closures on suit jackets with bungee cords.

- For a great bathrobe, cut a hole in the middle of a chenille bedspread and slip on over your head. Matching pillow sham makes a jaunty nightcap.
- Winter jacket too small? Run down to the basement and grab the quilted solar blanket off the water heater. Already equipped with strings to tie around you, it can be completed by merely adding a matching oven mitt as a hood. The protruding thumb should be worn to the side, like a tassel.
- Join the church choir and abscond with the robes (which, of course, you will later return, along with a generous donation to the roofing fund).
- Sew the ends of a hammock together for a nifty tube top.
- Cut two leg holes in a contour sheet for comfy, roomy underpants. Trim with a ruffled window valance for a sassy flair.

Of course, you'll be able to think of lots, lots more!

NINTH-MONTH
FASHION DOS AND DON'TS

- DO opt for the Basic Little Black Dress. Of course, now it will need to be the Basic GREAT BIG HUGE Black Dress. Good choice: Liz Claiborne's Nuns Line inspired by habits worn by the Sisters of Our Lady of Enormity.
- DON'T wear orange in your ninth month, especially in October. ("It's the Great Pumpkin, Charlie Brown!")

- DO accessorize. Bold earrings and necklaces draw attention away from your stomach and to your now-radiant face. For the look you want, consult TV listings for reruns of "The A-Team."
- DON'T wear purple. There's a vicious backlash of Barney haters out there who will shoot on sight.

STORKS ILLUSTRATED SWIMSUIT EDITION

Of all the indignities a pregnant woman suffers, the maternity swimsuit is perhaps the ultimate blow.

In search of a flattering style in swimwear for the pregnant woman, the best minds in fashion design got together to come up with a chic, discreet look for the mother-to-be. Unfortunately, while at this little get-together, they evidently took the opportunity to consume a staggering amount of scotch between turns at the drawing board. ("Let's make her look like a pheasant with a glandular problem." "No, I've got it—a sea nymph with an eating disorder!")

The result—evidently inspired by the billowy blouson look popularized by Shelley Winters in *The Poseidon Adventure*—is a fantasy-come-true for any woman who has ever dreamed of looking like a giant jellyfish.

On land you'll look like a manatee sunning itself. But in the water the blouson maternity suit redeems itself, rendering you not only fashionable but sea-worthy. As the water gets underneath the material, it billows out, allowing you to just lie back and bob about the waves as the "Baywatch" boys run up and down the beach flailing their arms and screaming at the children, "MAN-O'-WAR! GET OUT OF THE WATER! GET OUT OF THE WATER!!"

Elle MacPherson and Kathy Ireland, eat your hearts out.

IF THE SHOE FITS, IT'S A MIRACLE

Some experts tell women to expect their feet to grow by two shoe sizes. These experts, as you can imagine, have no female friends, leastwise any of childbearing age.

But don't blame the messenger. There is a good reason for your feet to grow. With the rest of you inflating to such impressive proportions, you need a more substantial base. Otherwise you would just topple over, crushing innocent passersby, causing untold damage and chaos.

To prevent this carnage and to prevent you from having to spend your third trimester on your face, Nature, in her wisdom, stepped in (so to speak) and programmed your foot hormones to go berserk.

So you'll need to locate shoes. Not just any shoes, mind you. Pregnant women are advised to wear "sensible, comfortable shoes." That is, in fact, good advice—in much the same way it is good advice to suggest that the people of Somalia eat healthy, well-balanced meals. The theory is sound, if impractical. Everyone *wants* to comply, but the question is *how*.

The woman with large, difficult-to-fit feet will soon discover the origins of the phrase "barefoot and pregnant." If, as a child, you suffered the humiliation of being told at skating rinks that the white skates wouldn't fit you and that you'd have to wear the *black* ones, shoes are now going to be a BIG problem.

Your quest to find shoes to accommodate your big swollen feet will become frenzied, eventually taking you to stores specializing in *oversized* women's shoes—places with names such as Ye Olde Gunboat Shoppe and Sasquatch R Us. Unfortunately, such stores stock only the ugliest of footwear, assuming that anyone having such enormous feet must be far too unattractive to appear in public at all.

SOLE SURVIVAL

Since regular stores can't help you, you'll have to expand your search. Try athletic shoe stores. Most of these stores employ adolescents who are unaccustomed to pregnant athletes, so whisper to the clerk that you're Shaquille O'Neal's sister and you've got a basketball under your dress.

Unfortunately, the clerk will likely comment (loudly) on the fact that you are trying on *men's* footwear and he's not sure that's allowed. He will then call over the manager to get authorization. The manager, annoyed at being interrupted from his algebra homework, will announce that he's pretty sure it's against company policy. He'll have to call the home office. Meanwhile, a crowd will gather and begin circling and staring as if you were recently un-earthed by a team of archaeologists.

You'll eventually give up and return home, ex-hausted and empty-handed. Too tired to cook, you'll order out for pizza. It will arrive at your home in a box emblazoned with the words BIG FOOT. Resist the impulse to relocate the hot mozzarella to the deliv-ery boy's head.

WELCOME TO FREDERICK'S OF DOLLYWOOD—MAY I HELP YOU?

You'll be able to continue wearing your current bras for a little while. But one day (a day that will forever burn itself into your memory) you will catch sight of yourself in the mirror. A look of stunned awe will cross your face—a look not unlike that of Roy Scheider as he watched the great white shark pass beside the boat in *Jaws*. Badly shaken, you will back from the mirror, steadying yourself against the door-jamb . . . *I think you're going to need a bigger bra.*

As you blossom from a size 32–Fried Egg to a 38-Popover, it will become all too apparent that those Victoria's Secret gossamer stretch-and-lace confec-tions aren't quite doing the job anymore.

It might be time to get a maternity bra when your current one:

- smooshes you like one of those tavern wenches in merrie olde England
- cannot be hooked without luggage strap extensions
- perches atop your breasts like twin party hats

Even if you are accustomed to going braless, you will eventually want to get a maternity bra. After all, even the most ardent supporters of nonsupport have their limits. You can only take so much bouncing and chafing; eventually a mere stroll across the room becomes a contact sport, and the facial bruises become increasingly hard to explain. ("I was walking along, minding my own business, and this breast comes flying out of *nowhere. . . .*")

Sure signals that it's past time for a trip to Victoria's Very *BIG* Secret:

1. People start asking about those rug burns on your knees.
2. You keep finding notes on your desk with the Battered Women's Hotline number.

But if you're still not sure, you can try a variation of the "pencil test"—a time-honored gauge used to determine the necessity of a bra in adolescence. In that test, you simply place a pencil under your breast, and if it stays put, you need a bra. If it falls to the floor, you don't.

The test is the same for maternity bras with one small adjustment—instead of a pencil, you'll be using a shovel.

Most maternity bras achieve support through the use of underwires and shelf brackets. This is a design borrowed from Las Vegas nightclub cigarette girls—that is, a sturdy shelf suspended from a strap around the neck and shoulders. ("No, you may not *pet* the Camels!")

These harnesses are not cheap. You might as well just go for broke and get a combo, one with detachable flaps for nursing, one that will accommodate your even bigger lactating breasts. ("Do you have that in a 44 long?")

The best maternity bras, however, are sophisticated engineering marvels—their design a collaborative effort of NASA and drunken Purdue undergrads. The industry leader is, of course, Frederick's of Lockheed, with its BOIIIIINNNNNGG-38DD, featuring reinforced steel fuselage and nose cones for lift and thrust when bounding upstairs. ("Uhhhh, that's a roger, Houston . . . we have liftoff.") They can also withstand the impact of fully loaded bombers reentering the atmosphere as you bound down the flight of stairs. ("Roger, Houston, this is Cantaloupe 2 . . . the melons have landed. The melons have landed.")

AFTER THE FALL

Because these maternity/nursing bra contraptions cost only slightly less than your monthly mortgage payment, you will want to make *some* use of them when they are no longer needed for bosom duty. With a little creativity, maternity bras can be used again and again! Try some of these helpful recycling tips:

• Maternity/nursing bras make dandy eco-conscious shopping bags. Detachable flap allows for easy, no-hands unloading.

- What backyard landscape wouldn't be enhanced by the Maternal Bird Feeder? Merely hang from a tree by its straps and fill cups with bird seed. A full year's supply! A favorite of Robin Red Breast. Audubon Society Save-a-Finch feature: Partially open a drop-down flap for a constant, measured stream of nourishment to your little feathered friends on the ground with broken wings.
- Take muffins, pastries, and other fragile baked goods to family gatherings in your handy new Muffin Tote with carrying straps. Crumb cleanup is quick and easy with the pull-down flap.
- Nursing bra cups make great knee bandages, accommodating even the knobbiest of joints during bending and squatting. Just tape on and go. With the nursing flap, there'll be no more skin-ripping adhesive ordeals every time you want to take a peek.
- Starch the cups heavily and use as cereal bowls. Your husband can get his Kix in the morning while you breast-feed baby.
- Donate a bra to the carnival sideshow as feed bags for the two-headed cow.
- No more fighting at twins' birthday parties when you can have a double pinata! Fill maternity bra cups with candy and hang from the ceiling. Tie a breast pump to a broomstick and watch the fun.
- Save up nursing bras from your neighbors and friends. When you've collected twenty, you've got enough to make a giant Advent calendar for parochial school gymnasiums. Imagine the delight on a

child's face as he pulls down the flap to discover the day's surprise!

- More holiday fun! At the office Christmas party, gather your friends and line them up to form a Living Twelve Days of Christmas tableau. You, of course, take up position in the eleventh slot—maids a-milking.

WHAT TO DO WITH THE REST OF THOSE MATERNITY CLOTHES

- Don't throw away those maternity slacks! Stretch them across your backyard, tying the legs to opposite trees and positioning the stretch tummy panel in the center. The neighborhood kids will flock to your new trampolines!
- Maternity underpants make dandy snoods for Weber barbecues.
- No more fighting over the covers or yanking them off your spouse at night! Cut out the stretch tummy panels from all your slacks and skirts. Stitch together to make a one-size-fits-all patchwork quilt.
- Maternity shorts make clever appliance covers for your side-by-side washer and dryer.
- A colorful circle skirt, heavily starched, makes a terrific patio umbrella.
- Dress up a powder room and hide unsightly under-sink plumbing with one of your elastic-waist maternity skirts. Just slice down the back and attach to the sink with double-stick tape. Stand back and wait for the compliments.

- Perk up any bedroom! Just shorten elastic-waist maternity skirts and stretch over the box spring for a brand new dust ruffle.
- Heavily starch a striped maternity smock for a snappy new porch awning.
- Backyard camp-outs are a cinch for the kiddies with a maternity tent dress draped over a pole. Bonus: little fingers won't get burned while making s'mores—dress shields are right at hand, ready for pot holder duty.

7

Exercise During Pregnancy

Hahahahahahahahahahahahaha

Many people will tell you that it is important to maintain a regular schedule of exercise so that you do not get Out of Shape. It should be noted that they are not talking about your Present Shape. The shape they are referring to is the Pregnant Shape, which resembles the state of Missouri.

If you are accustomed to exercise, simply continue what you've been doing, making just a few minor concessions to your condition. For example, if you're accustomed to morning aerobics on the TV with those peppy, energetic people on the beach, merely change the channel to something less vigorous—such as

- the traveler's forecast on the Weather Channel
- "Mr. Rogers' Neighborhood"
- Willard Scott on the "Today" show displaying pictures of centenarians wearing party hats

And don't forget to use that mute button on the remote control!

Generally, the only reason anyone endures an exercise regime is to see tangible results of the effort—for example, a flat stomach. So, unless you find it gratifying to measure your progress with *increased* inches, exercise during pregnancy may turn out to be a tad disappointing.

You may also find that exercise during pregnancy is even more uncomfortable than it was before due to the fact that there is now a baby inside you wedging its elbows and knees into your rib cage while doing its own aerobic routine on your bladder.

If you're not sure this is for you, here are some prepregnancy exercises you can do to simulate what it will be like to workout while With Child:

- First, drink a gallon of water. Then strap a twenty-pound bag of potting soil around your waist (to which you've added one medium-sized house pet) and jog in place for thirty minutes.
- Eat an entire Thanksgiving dinner. For dessert, order an extra-large pizza. Wash it down with several milk shakes. Then climb the stairs to the top of the Empire State Building.
- Third-trimester sit-ups can be simulated by situating yourself on your back underneath John Goodman.

DRESSING THE PART

But what will I wear, you ask? You will be pleased to know that Lycra spandex—a fabric you were reluctant to wear when your figure was only slightly im-perfect—now comes in maternity sizes! This triumph of modern science came about during USDA research aimed at shrink-wrapping livestock.

Yes, ladies, now you exercising preggos need no longer hide behind those baggy gray sweats. Imagine yourself in shimmery electric-blue or Day-Glo acid green, side by side with those perky little size-5 people cavorting in front of a mirrored wall. As the Mother Superior counseled the nuns as they entered the ca-sino to save Whoopi Goldberg in *Sister Act,* "Try to blend in."

Yes, you'll blend right in—in much the same way Charles Barkley blends in on the streets of Beijing.

And don't worry about the children who point and squeal. They are not making fun of you; they are merely expressing their delight, just as they would if they had spotted any Mylar balloon cartoon charac-ter that had just blown off its moorings in the Macy's parade.

SWEATIN' TO THE OLDIES
IN STRETCHED-OUT UNDIES

If public displays do not appeal to you, there are al-ways exercise shows on TV featuring chirpy-voiced, muscular individuals who will exhort you to join in the fun as they bounce and stretch and jump and march and flex and just basically annoy the hell out of you at the crack of dawn.

Be aware, however, that such shows can exacer-bate morning sickness. In fact, many people who aren't even pregnant find themselves running for the bathroom while tuned in to these shows. Don't you just want to SLAP them? ("That's it! You got it!! March it out now! Bring it on up and take it on down!! Work through that pain!") You can join in the fun as soon as you quit heaving your guts out.

You will, however, get lots of exercise screaming obscenities and throwing spoiled produce at the TV screen.

Videos are perhaps a better option for exercise in the privacy of your own home. Since your mental health is as important as your physical health at this time, it is best to avoid videos put out by Victoria Principal or Cindy Crawford. In fact, any woman in her right mind will avoid these videos.

Some better video choices:

- *The Pillsbury Doughboy Workout*
- *National Geographic's Rolling with the Humpbacked Whales*
- John Candy's *Buns of Steel*

Better yet, forget the videos and exercise to music only. Good bets:

- "Sixteen Tons"—Tennessee Ernie Ford
- "Elephant Walk"—Donald Jenkins
- "I Am the Walrus"—the Beatles

And, of course, anything by Fats Domino, Chubby Checker, or Meat Loaf.

FOR PREGGOS ONLY . . .

There are, of course, videos put out specifically for pregnant women. These, however, should also be avoided, because none of the women featured are really pregnant. Their tiny behinds, thighs, calves, and ankles give them away and are signals that the oversized "belly" they sport is, in fact, the result of special effects created under the direction of Steven Spielberg.

(*Note:* For health reasons, it must be mentioned that the letters *VCR* are prime components in the words *varicose veins.*)

For you history buffs, Pregnant Woman Workouts became popular after a gathering in Amsterdam of the world's foremost Elderly Male Obstetrical Authorities. They unanimously agreed that with modern technology, pregnancy was becoming far less grueling than it should be.

What better way to reverse this trend than to come up with an exercise program for preggos? They needed an expert spokesperson. Taking another hit off the hookah, they all agreed that the most qualified person should be a thrice-married war protester turned actress turned movie mogul wife whose gynecological/gymnastic expertise was well documented in such films as *Barbarella* and *Klute.*

(*Note:* All exercise videos should be rented and not purchased. You will understand why after your first workout.)

Many health clubs, spas, and hospitals have added workout classes solely for pregnant women. The advantage of these classes is that the instructors aren't nearly as perky, which has been the case ever since that rash of Pregasize instructor lynchings. (You might remember the newspaper accounts—six women were tried and acquitted for hanging their bouncy, PEPPY instructor, Candi Sue, with an umbilical cord. After the jury saw a videotape of the classes, the case was ruled justifiable homicide.)

There you can line up with dozens of other preggos just like you! Arrayed in blinding fluorescent shades of green, orange, and blue, you sway and stretch to the music—a surreal Fantasia where irradiated watermelons come to life on the hillside of Chernobyl.

REAL EXERCISES FOR REAL PREGGOS

There is no point in actually going to an exercise studio to engage in unpleasant invigorating activity when you can get tons of exercise just by being pregnant. Here is a sampling of exercises that Nature herself has devised for the expectant mother.

FIRST TRIMESTER

Aerobic Phone Dialing to Spread the
  News
100-Yard Dash for the Bathroom
Early-Morning Toilet Seat Lift
In-the-Bed Saltine Crunches
After-Eight Heavy-Eyelid Raises
Power Walking through the Mall's Baby
  Department
Fluctuating-Hormone Mood Lunges

SECOND TRIMESTER

Ben & Jerry's Three-Scoop Rocky Road Waffle
  Cone Lift
Thick-Crust Sausage and Mushroom Marathon
Baby Name Tug-of-War
Hemorrhoid Push-Ups
Decorating the Nursery Budget Stretch

THIRD TRIMESTER

During the latter stages of pregnancy, many women
find that merely attempting to get up out of a chair
can be an exhausting workout. However, true exercise
nuts will enjoy adding the following to their routine:

Getting Out of the Bathtub
Putting on Pantyhose
Lactating-Breast Hoist
Can't-Find-a-Rest-Room Bladder Squeeze
Power-Lifting Shower Gifts into the Car
Two-Week-Overdue Exercise in Patience

TOUGHENING YOUR NIPPLES:
TRAINING YOUR BREASTS TO BE LUNCH

Breast-feeding should be a warm, bonding, pleasur-
able activity for you and baby. But, if you are unpre-
pared, your initial efforts may not meet these lofty
expectations. Because up until now, the most grueling challenge your nipples have had to face involved

a malfunctioning spray nozzle at the Holiday Inn.

So unless you are a member of a tribe whose beauty rituals include hubcaps dangling from fourteen-carat-gold posts in your nipples, your nipples are out of shape and will need to be trained and toughened for breast-feeding.

The idea is, you see, to desensitize the little nodules so that when the baby is feeding you can act nonchalant in restaurants and airplanes, as if you didn't notice there was a small person attached to your breast. A barnacle in a bonnet.

The conventional advice is to, several times a day during pregnancy, roll the nipple between thumb and forefinger while pulling gently outward as if you were tuning in a shortwave radio. However, this can be distracting to your co-workers.

There are several discreet training alternatives:

1. Line your bra with steel wool and go jogging.
2. Keep a snapping turtle in your bathtub.
3. Remove the suction cups from any "BABY ON BOARD" car window sign and attach them to your nipples with Super Glue. After several days, rip them off.
4. While doing your morning makeup, let that eyelash curler do double duty.

8

Old Wives' Tales

Would Grandma Lie?

Nothing attracts old wives' tales like a pregnant woman. Many people insist that these questionable bits of folk wisdom have their origins in truth; these people will, in fact, get their knickers in a knot if you suggest otherwise. They *know* they're true, because Great Great Grandma Winifred told Great Grandma Clarice, who told Great Aunt Zenobia (who never had children of her own and wore a slip on her head most of the time) that she thought it sounded about right.

Who are you to argue with such unimpeachable sources?

Actually, old wives' tales date back to ancient times, a period known to be heavily populated with ancient people—hence the term *ancient times*. Consequently, most of the wives were pretty old. (Because of shorter life expectancies caused by such things as lax animal control ordinances and unrefrigerated meat, women qualified as old wives just by surviving puberty.)

Cave paintings found in what is now Cleveland clearly depict a woman in labor being attended by what appears to be another woman in desperate need of electrolysis. Archaeologists believe this is evidence of the existence of old wives. A clue to the nature of their role and counsel occurs in the chiseled inscription—"arruuurrrghhurrrgh"—which represents the sum total of obstetrical advice at the time. ("Hurry up. We need the afterbirth for the harvest festival decorations.")

BOY OR GIRL?
DO-IT-YOURSELF ULTRASOUND

Predicting the sex of the child was a strong suit among old wives of ancient times, and even today it remains their specialty. But because of equal opportunity laws and age and sex discrimination statutes, such prognostications are no longer the sole province of old wives. Anyone can play!

All sorts of helpful friends, along with people you have never met, will suddenly become baby soothsayers, unerring predictors of the sex of your child. They will stream toward you like pilgrims to a shrine, in an endless caravan, each bearing her own mystical method, each guaranteed to be THE absolutely positively never-fail foolproof way to tell if it's a boy or a girl.

Most of these people, in real life, are intelligent,

logical human beings who hold down jobs, vote, and dress themselves. However, when a pregnant woman comes into range, she evidently radiates some sort of powerful lunatic hormone that penetrates their skulls and turns their minds to mush.

They will enumerate the hundreds of successful predictions they've made. Never mind that an ultrasound test can do this with 100 percent accuracy. They will assure you that never *once* have they been wrong—except, of course, for that one time with Ida-Lou Weidermuth's baby, which inexplicably turned out to be a boy instead of a girl—*but* even now, sixteen years later, it's starting to look like the prediction was right after all, *if you know what we mean.*

They will insist that you try their astoundingly accurate method right then and there. Never mind that you're standing in line at the cafeteria—let's just move this ketchup and wipe this little bit of Thousand Island off this empty table, whaddya say?

If you attempt to decline politely, they will take personal offense. They will act as if you had accused them of witchcraft. If you are lucky, they will gather up their newt eyes and frog toes and leave in a huff, scurrying off to gossip about you with the rest of the coven.

Turn down any sex-guessing offers from strangers. Be polite, because they may be serial killers, but be firm. Tell them you already know it's a boy (or a girl) because *you* happen to be psychic, and by the way, is there someone in their life whose name starts with a *J* that wants to kill them? Check on this.

However, relatives, friends, and co-workers require more tact—they will hold it against you for the rest of your life if you don't eagerly sign on for their pet techniques. They'll make up stories about you involving tattooed carnival workers with random tooth placement. Or they'll wait until your child is born, then deliberately saddle it with some odious nickname such as Booger or Babycakes, which will, down the road, eliminate any chance of a salaried position.

So it is important to humor these people. Indulge their little medieval quirks. Remember, these people will make up the guest list for many of your baby showers! ("Why, yes, I'd *love* to be sprinkled with raven's blood. Could we do it now, right here in the elevator?")

Since there are, at this writing, only two sexes from which to choose, many of their methods will in fact be accurate—roughly, a mind-boggling 50 percent of the time.

Here are a few of the more popular methods used to determine the sex of your baby:

THE HANDWRITING-ON-THE-WALL METHOD

A pencil hung from string dangled over your belly has astounding power to tell whether you are carrying a boy or a girl. In addition to the dandy applications for pregnant women, this talent for discerning between the sexes makes the lowly pencil an invaluable dating aid for naive men when visiting bars in unfamiliar neighborhoods. ("Pardon me, but before we writhe to the beat on the dance floor, I'd like to suspend my Faber-Castell number two over your stomach.")

The method goes like this: First tie a pencil to a string. Then lie on your back while a friend suspends the string steady, pencil point down, over your belly.

As the folklore goes, the sex of the child will reveal itself as you observe the direction in which the pencil moves. Of course, no one ever remembers just what means a boy and what means a girl, so you're likely to have this performed on you several times with disparate conclusions, and a fight will break out among rival factions. It's an argument that cannot be resolved until you actually have the baby and prove one of them right.

Unfortunately, you will also prove one of them wrong. Being responsible for this person's now-less-than-perfect accuracy record—a far more egregious affront than merely refusing the test in the first place—you will be punished with a flurry of rumor and innuendo regarding the way in which you conducted your pregnancy and, sad to say, your life in general (which may or may not include reference to the aforementioned Tilt-a-Whirl operator).

Some people swear that if the pencil starts moving in a circular motion, it indicates a boy. If it sways back and forth, it indicates a girl. Others will tell you the exact opposite. Getting the pencil practitioners to settle on this is about as likely as Michael Jackson settling on a nose.

What they do agree on, however, is that you *must* use a plain old regular desk pencil. If, like Boy George's mother, you use an eyebrow pencil, you won't be able to tell *which* way it swings.

If the pencil sways *and* swirls, you could be having twins. Or it could mean that your friend is drunk. Just to be sure, ask her to suspend her car keys over the hood of the car. If *she* sways, call a cab.

MR. WIZARD MEETS
JOSEPHINE THE PLUMBER

Other sex-predicting aficionados prefer a scientific approach, employing science-related activities similar (but not identical) to those favored by scientists.

So, your more analytical friends will likely want to do sophisticated chemistry tests on you, such as adding drain cleaner to a cup of your urine. The resulting color supposedly tells you the sex of the baby. (More important, it tells you to exercise extreme caution when offered a beverage in this person's home.)

If the concoction bubbles over and creates a gaping hole in your countertop, this says less about the *sex* of the child than it does about its *temperament.* You might wish to consult an exorcist.

HOW ARE YOU CARRYING IT?
TELLING A BOOK BY ITS COVER

Many people claim that merely observing the way you carry your baby is the most accurate way of determining sex. (This is, of course, almost foolproof after the baby is born, when the presence of pink ribbons and lacy bonnets offers additional clues.)

If you are carrying your baby low, that supposedly indicates you're going to have a boy. The rationale for this evidently originated with observations on the manner in which an adult male carries his own belly—low, balanced precariously on a huge Coors belt buckle.

If you are carrying "out front," that's another clue you will have a boy. If you are carrying in a more all-around fashion, suspect a girl, who is evidently getting a head start at taking over the household, getting into your closets and drawers and lounging about, stretching the umbilical cord around the corner as she lies on your bladder with her feet up on your pancreas.

Stomach shapes come into play too. Is your belly shaped like a football? Congratulations; it's a boy! More like a basketball? Congratulations, it's a girl! This is not as sexist as it sounds. It is, in fact, a scientific determination. Football=NFL; basketball= NBA. Translation: No Female Likely and Not Boy Apparently.

MIRROR, MIRROR ON THE WALL . . .

Some people insist that they can tell if you are carrying a boy or a girl just from observing your facial features. The mothers of boys, the theory goes, can be recognized by their exceptional beauty. This, of course, is pure nonsense. (For evidence of this, consult photographs of Eleanor Roosevelt, mother of five sons.)

Still, what's the harm in someone guessing you're going to have a boy if the guess is based on your startling beauty? You will, of course, concur with the conclusion. ("Yup, sounds right to me. Amazing system you've got there.")

Unless the person doing the guessing has the brains of a herring, she will always guess that, from your looks, it's gonna be a boy. Because the flip side of this guessing game is the endearing notion that the mothers of girls become plain, if not downright butt-ugly. So if someone says you look like you're carrying a girl and you haven't yet tossed your cookies this morning, now's the time. ("Oh, I'm so sorry! Was that silk?")

The baby girl, you see, is said to suck out all her mother's beauty for herself. Presumably this is done via the umbilical cord in much the same way you would siphon gas out of a pickup truck. Either this is pure poppycock, or mothers like Naomi Judd have figured out a way to sabotage the system.

SELECT-A-SEX TECHNIQUES

Since ultrasound is rapidly running these uterine psychics out of business, many of them are diversifying, expanding their repertoire of old wives' tales to include helpful hints on how you can determine the sex of your child. They are eager to share these hints with you. In fact they are *compelled* to share them with you. Typically they will do this in a public place.

Some of their suggestions must be implemented during conception, which means, of course, that these people will be giving you step-by-step directions on how they want you to have (sssshhh!) intercourse. You are not supposed to notice this. You are supposed to act as if you are being given directions on how to repot a geranium or unclog a sink trap.

You will be told that the sex of the child always matches that of the dominant partner in lovemaking. Obviously, this information will never be volunteered by a man with six daughters.

If nothing else, this could offer entertaining possibilities at social gatherings. The Mr. Milquetoast next door with four boys might not be such a wuss after all. And how about Joe Jock Studd across the street with his three girls? Lots you don't know about his shy little mousy wife, huh?

Or, it could only confirm what you already suspected. Note the sex of Bill and Hillary Clinton's only child.

Other methods, to be effective, must be applied throughout pregnancy. This approach presumes that baby just lies there, waiting for external stimuli and clues as to which direction it should go. ("Boy? Girl? Boy? Girl? Decisions, decisions. I can't take the pressure!") So you must help it come to a decision.

Old wives suggest that, if you want a boy, you lie on your right side while sleeping. Evidently this will apply pressure to strategic areas, cutting off blood flow and preventing the formation of certain organs, encouraging the production of others.

(*WARNING:* Sleeping on your back can result in babies who grow up to be Pat on "Saturday Night Live.")

Some old wives insist that the sex of your next child can be predicted even before conception. Simply observe your current child. If its first word was *Mama*, you can safely decorate the nursery pink. If it says "Dada," start mixing the blue paint. If it says "helter-skelter," go with black—a cave motif, perhaps.

Of course, all bets are off if you have a foreign nanny.

MORE TALES FROM THE CRYPTIC

• *TAKE LARGE DAILY DOSES OF COD LIVER OIL AND OLIVE OIL, AND YOUR DELIVERY WILL BE EASY. THE BABY WILL SLIP RIGHT OUT.* Evidently the birth canal operates like an anatomical Slip 'n' Slide. Unfortunately, cod liver oil and olive oil cannot tell the difference between birth canals and other outlets. Nor can they distinguish between your baby and your lunch. So, for the nine months leading up to the effortless event of baby's slipping right out, everything else will be slipping out as well. For similar results without the side effects, you might try WD-40 in place of your feminine hygiene spray. Or substitute Oil of Olay— not only will baby slip right out; it won't be wrinkled!

- *DON'T REACH UP, OR THE UMBILICAL CORD WILL CREEP UP AND STRANGLE THE BABY.* No one really believes this. It just keeps getting repeated for the same reasons people keep telling that slumber party story about kids necking in their car while a homicidal maniac with a hook was on the loose. (They drive away, and later they find . . . a—gasp—*hook* . . . on the driver's side door. Nyahhahaha!)

  Actually, this apocryphal notion about babies being strangled with umbilical cords is the result of the March 12, 1872, *Sweetwater Sun Gazette*, which ran a story about a benevolent Mexican rancher and his adopted sons entitled "Umberto Cordero's Baby Wranglers." Unfortunately, the only literate person in Sweetwater at the time broke his glasses only moments before climbing the bandstand to read the Gazette to the gathered townspeople, many of whom were, coincidentally, old wives.

- *PERMS YOU GET DURING PREGNANCY WON'T HOLD.* Evidently raging pregnal hormones attack the perm's curl activator molecules, changing the chemical composition to something resembling battery acid, which, instead of curling your hair, will turn it to cotton candy. This is, in fact, precisely the method used by the manufacturers of Troll doll hair and, incidentally, Don King.

  The foremost minds in cosmetology are, however, working on a revolutionary new perm for pregnant women, and clinical trials are under way on the promising new formula, which will be packaged under the brand name S'perm.

- *ACCORDING TO ENGLISH SUPERSTITION, BIG EARS ARE GOOD LUCK.* Well, *of course* they're going to say this! You think they're going to say anything that isn't nice about big ears, what with Prince Charles always lurking about? Actually, he *did* have the good fortune to be born into royalty, which is pretty lucky as those things go, considering the perks, which include palaces and mistresses and all the Yorkshire pudding he can eat, so perhaps the tale is true in England anyway.

- *YOU LOSE A TOOTH FOR EVERY CHILD.* If this were true, nine out of ten dentists would recommend, in their guidelines for healthy teeth and gums, a schedule of checkups, flossing, and regular use of Crest with Spermicide.

    Priests would be able to tell at a glance who the good Catholics were among the new parishioners. ("I can't help but notice your full set of teeth, Mrs. O'Malley. Say three Hail Marys and return in nine months—and you'd better have a molar missing.")

- *DON'T GET DENTAL FILLINGS WHILE YOU'RE PREGNANT, BECAUSE THEY'LL FALL OUT.* While dentists claim that this old wives' tale is completely false, there may be a grain of truth to it. It is not the pregnancy that causes the fillings to fall out, however. Exhaustive research has turned up a case in England where a woman lost a filling during her lengthy, painful labor in which she was biting down on a washcloth. Seized by a particularly bad contraction, she slipped, coming down on her husband's finger, severing it at the second joint, and knocking out her filling. (Presumably neither of these two Brits had big ears.)

- *A PREGNANT WOMAN'S NOSE GETS BIGGER.* Sadly, there is some truth to this. Your body is beefing up its blood supply, so capillaries and veins swell. Since your nose is just full of these things, it will swell too. One presumes there is some other explanation for Karl Malden and Bill Clinton.

- *BIRTHMARKS ARE CAUSED BY A FRIGHT TO THE MOTHER DURING PREGNANCY.* Unless you want your child to look like a Jackson Pollock painting, lay off the Dean Koontz novels.

- *BIRTHMARKS ARE ACTUALLY STORK BITES.* This has been traced back to an old wives' tale started by Ann Rice's great aunt, who never did find a publisher for her chilling novel *Interview with the Stork.*

     One cannot be entirely sure if it is the bite itself that causes the mark or, as suggested by proponents of the fear theory just discussed, the fright to the mother that is responsible.

     Fear is a natural reaction anytime a pointy-billed bird the size of a Shetland pony swoops into the delivery room, snapping at you, intent on biting something. However, today our modern building codes and sturdy roofs limit access and have all but eliminated these fly-by bitings. So there's no cause for alarm, unless, of course, you plan on giving birth in an area without roofs, such as Haiti.

9
Life in a
Fishbowl

The Communal Pregnancy

STEP RIGHT UP, FOLKS!

Although pregnancy and childbirth have been going on for quite some time now—as far back as, oh, the Middle Ages at least (probably longer)—the novelty still has not worn off. People are fascinated by pregnant women and, despite the relative frequency of the condition, still react as if the circus were in town.

Indeed, a unicorn horn protruding from your forehead would garner less attention than your pregnant belly. And certainly fewer nosy questions.

Even sideshow attractions are accorded some measure of control over the sightseers. They schedule specific hours of operation, no one gets in without an admission ticket, and there are strict rules governing visitors' behavior while viewing patrons. DO NOT TOUCH THE TWO-HEADED COW!! DO NOT PET IGUANA WOMAN!

These rules of etiquette, however, do not apply to encounters with pregnant people. You see, as a preggo you are no longer a private citizen. You are now a National Treasure, a tourist attraction not unlike the Grand Canyon, the Statue of Liberty, or Graceland. You are a mobile museum exhibit, a Magical Mystery Tour drawing a steady flow of curiosity seekers who, not content simply to peer and stare, will behave as if you were a petting zoo.

Complete strangers who apologize profusely should they accidentally brush their handbag on your shopping cart and who take great pains to avoid the slightest elbow contact in an elevator will now march straight up to you and pat your belly as if it were a cocker spaniel.

People you have never met before, many of whom fall into the category of People Who Should Remain Unmet, will appear out of nowhere, palms front, making a beeline for your belly. In the mall, in the supermarket, in the parking lot—they will gather around you like travel-weary vagrants warming their hands at a potbellied stove.

Three out of seven of these people will have one or more of the following characteristics: hacking cough, body odor, halitosis, fever blisters, eczema, and a minimum of four filthy, fraying Band-Aids on their outstretched fingers.

Every now and then you will be accosted at a convenience store by a particularly unnerving character—usually someone with psychotic red hair and one wandering eye—who will insist on "blessing" your child and making a prediction regarding its destiny. Pointing a finger heavenward, she prophesies: "It is written that a little child shall be born of a woman bearing groceries, and he shall wear the number 7-Eleven on his forehead."

SECURITY MEASURES

The wise preggo will take steps to protect herself. However, most available feminine protection is useless for the pregnant woman. It is not enough to menacingly brandish a maxi-pad or to carry a can of feminine hygiene spray. ("One step closer and you're fresh as a morning breeze, sucker!")

What women need is serious protection. Consider the following:

BIG MAMA WARNING SYSTEM

Similar to a car alarm, the device is equipped with sensors that detect approaching intruders, warning them away with flashing lights, sirens, and a computerized voice command. "WHOOP-WHOOP-WHOOP-WHOOP!! YOU ARE TOO CLOSE TO THE UTERUS! STEP BACK FROM THE UTERUS! WHOOP-WHOOP-WHOOP-WHOOP!!!"

BUSYBODY REPELLENT

Similar to Mace, the active ingredient in this aerosol spray is testosterone. One spritz of the male hormone, and the busybody will be stopped in her tracks, paralyzed and repulsed by the very thought of discussing "female" stuff.

BODYGUARDS

Surround yourself with large surly-looking women who will stand about with their arms crossed, scowling and blocking access to your tummy. Try to find women who resemble Anne Ramsey or Dick Butkus.

Don't underestimate the power of words, either. You can mount an effective defense against uterine space invaders with your superior intellect and verbal skills. Examples:

- "What is this—Tailhook? Getcher stinkin' hands OFF me!"
- "Why, no, I'm not pregnant actually. It's a rare tumor caused by an incurable virus. Did I mention it's contagious?"
- "I'm just carrying it for a friend."
- "Careful, it's a bomb."

The constant attention and solicitous behavior of even good friends and relatives will eventually wear thin. If *one more* person asks you when your due date is, you'll go for the throat. They mean well, and you can't be rude—well, you could, but there are those baby showers to consider—so the best thing you can do is derive some entertainment value from it. Tell everyone a different due date. At five months, say you're due any day. If you're eight months pregnant, tell them you have six months to go.

And no matter how long you've been married, people will count back the months. If you're due in February, and you were married in September, there will be plenty of raised eyebrows. That this particular September occurred in 1985 is beside the point.

No one knows just why friends and relatives react with such surprise when they see you pregnant. Perhaps it's because up until now it had not occurred to them that you might actually be engaging in baby-making activities.

Or maybe it's just the shock of seeing your face on Rush Limbaugh's body.

For example, a chance encounter with someone you have not seen for a year could go something like this:

Friend catches sight of you waddling across the street and struggling to make it up the curb. She rushes toward you, grabs you by the shoulders, and squeals: "You're PREGNANT!!!" at which time you look down at your belly, an expression of shock and horror crossing your face. "Holy $%#@, you're right! Stay calm. Nobody move."

LET ME GIVE YOU
A LITTLE ADVICE, HONEY . . .

You might as well just resign yourself to the attention. Your condition, it seems, places you in the public domain. If this disturbs you, *get over it*. You are now merely a vessel, Carrier of the Communal Baby.

You are, after all, only the mother in Everyone's Pregnancy, and for the next nine months you will be receiving more unsolicited comments than a contestant on "The Price Is Right."

Drink lots of apple juice. No, drink goat milk. Never drink sassafras tea. Always do this. Never do that. They will be watching you, too . . . waiting for you to slip up, keeping track, keeping score. Having a Coke with lunch? *I don't think so, young lady. Waiter, bring her a nice glass of milk, and, oh, by the way, cancel this lady's cheeseburger order and bring her a nice cottage cheese plate, OK?*

The Preggo Police will be out in force, skulking about, rifling your desk for forbidden snacks, snatching Snickers bars from your mouth and stuffing you with carrots. While everyone else is raving about the cappuccino, you'll be handed a nice glass of spring water. (The word *nice* is always used to define whatever it is they're trying to pass off as an acceptable substitute for what it is you really want, e.g., you'll be given a *nice* cup of herbal tea, a *nice* stalk of celery, a *nice* saltine cracker, etc.)

And when the Preggo Police aren't on patrol, you've got family, friends, co-workers, and complete and utter strangers who will delight in sharing with you the most intimate details of *their* pregnancies.

Because something very odd happens when a woman becomes pregnant. It's as if an eerie fog rolls in from some dark corner of the planet, where taste and decorum and modesty are unknown to the inhabitants. As the mist settles and envelops your unwitting companions, it neutralizes all previously held notions about what is proper subject matter for polite conversation, erasing from their minds any limits or inhibitions.

Other than that, they will act perfectly normal. You won't notice anything different. Everything will seem as it was. Until the topic turns to pregnancy.

Then you'll notice.

The very same people who, just last week, became nervous and flustered when a hemorrhoid ointment commercial aired during a mixed-company get-together will now be swapping detailed sagas of their own hemorrhoids (which, by the way, they named—each one individually, after congressmen, alphabetically, beginning with states starting with the letter *A* and ending, mercifully, with the letter *L*).

The same people who, just last month, got up and walked out when the conversation about Mexican vacations turned to talk of Montezuma's revenge will now be sharing involved chronologies of their own bowel habits during pregnancy.

Most men, however—especially men who happen to be your father or your boss—seem to be largely unaffected by this brain-altering fog and will not want to participate. While they may sit still and nod and emit unintelligible sympathetic-type sounds for a little while, eventually enough is enough. They'll bolt for the exits and leave skid marks in the parking lot when the conversation turns to mucous plugs.

TALES FROM THE TRENCHES

If such conversation strikes you as indelicate, well, it's gonna be a long nine months.

Because *none* of the people who so graciously offer to share their stories or advice have any idea that you might consider their stories indelicate. Of course, few will admit to having had normal, uneventful, joyous pregnancies. Oh, no. *Their* pregnancies were complex, dangerous ordeals, riddled with rare complications too involved and complicated to enumerate.

But they will enumerate them anyway. At great length, and in exquisite, horrid detail.

For the next nine months, every sentence they will utter will begin with the words "Well, when *I* was pregnant . . ."

Yes, it's that time. Time for the Battle of the Preggos, the Tournament of Wombs. Like veterans gathered at the Legion Hall swapping war stories, every conversation is a skirmish in the war of one-upmanship.

WOMAN #1: "You had morning sickness for three months? Honey, it never *stopped* with me. Why, I was upchucking the ice chips during labor."

WOMAN #2: "*My* morning sickness was so bad we got evicted for flushing the toilet so much."

WOMAN #3: "Yeah, well, at least you didn't have the dry heaves. *That's* the worst, I'm here to tell ya. I got stretch marks on top of my stretch marks—that's how violent they were. Tore my guts up."

WOMAN #1: "Stretch marks? You wanna talk stretch marks? I'll show you stretch marks." (She lifts her blouse up around her neck.)

WOMAN #2: (lifting her blouse) "See these? My kid
thinks I got run over by a tractor.
Likes to roll his Tonka trunk along the
tread marks . . . isn't that cute?"

There will be competitions.

- BEST BIG BOOB STORY: "I was never so embarrassed in all my life! The nerve of those people,
dragging me off to Security like that—like I would
even *want* to shoplift their lousy Gouda cheese
balls."

- BEST BIG BELLY STORY: "Finally, the *rescue
squad* had to get me out of the tub. They slathered
me with cooking oil, all the while shouting, 'Free
Willy! Free Willy!' "

- BEST WATER-BREAKING STORY: "So there I
was, speaking before the committee, and the chair-
man says, 'Madam, your arguments simply don't
hold water. . . .' "

Not having children does not disqualify a woman
from participation in this little ritual, either. Nay,
nay. It merely makes the process more of a challenge.
Childless women will appropriate the stories of relatives and friends. Unencumbered by direct first-
hand knowledge of the facts, they will tell stories
that are graphic and disgusting but also bizarre.
("And *then*, it turned out not to be a baby at all, but a
sixteen-pound *dermoid* with teeth and hair and, well,
the doctors swore it growled at them when they removed it.")

KODAK MOMENTS

And, of course, there's the traditional exchange of ultrasound photographs among pregnant women. One by one they'll be passed around the table. Although *your* ultrasound will be the clearest intrauterine snapshot ever taken, unmistakably showing the finest-looking child that ever swam in a sac, *theirs* . . . Oh, dear.

Locating the little tyke becomes a challenging game of "Where's Waldo?"

The protocol for these events demands that you *not* say what you're thinking. Words are unnecessary. A gasp of wonder and/or a mere squeal of delight is sufficient.

Refrain from observing that the child resembles a Doppler weather map indicating a storm front moving across the Great Plains. They could be satellite pictures of the Milky Way for all you know, but if *she* wants to think it's a baby, well, what's the harm?

Observations regarding family resemblance at this point are risky. ("I see he has his father's eyes." "Those are gallstones. The baby's over here.")

Nor is it wise to attempt to point out what you believe to be the child's various limbs and parts.

YOU: "Why, there's his little wee-wee!"

HER: (icily) "That's his foot."

YOU: "Wait a minute, wait a minute, there it is. Holy moly! Is that kid *hung*!"

HER: "*That* is the umbilical cord."

IS NOTHING SACRED?

After many months of this you too will begin to join in, dropping your defenses, starting to share *your* gross little tales with the gang.

Uh-uh. NOT ME! you say. Yes, you, dear.

Believe it or not, eventually you too will gather in the kitchen with friends to share, in graphic detail, every unappetizing aspect of your pregnancy. Numbed by the relentless barrage of utter frankness and stripped of all sense of propriety, ultimately you will succumb, entering into the world of No Limits, jumping in to top each dramatic testimonial with your own (better) story.

Nothing's beyond the pale. Enormous blood clots? Okeydokey! Plopping a piece of raw liver onto the counter, you crow triumphantly, "There. Imagine this about ten times bigger. With thorns."

But don't blame yourself. You won't be able to help it. It's the fog. Besides, it is all perfectly normal, merely nature's way of relieving you of your inhibitions to prepare you for the time when twenty-two different people will be peering at your crotch.

But no matter how blasé you get about this, do not, under any circumstances, agree to a cadre of friends and family and camcorders in the delivery room with you. They will, of course, clamor for the opportunity to "be there for you" and "support" you, but for most women it's sufficient that their friends "be there" for them in the context of doing lunch.

And even if you should take leave of your senses and allow a camcorder in the room, just whom might you show these films to? The neighbors? ("Come on over Saturday. We'll barbecue, tip a few, and watch Norma grunting like a warthog.") Certainly the child itself will not appreciate this later on. ("Mom, I swear if you drag out that tape for the prom party, I'll . . . .")

And what if you were to accidentally drop it off with your other rental tapes by mistake? They'd reshelve it, and some poor schmuck would come home with it, planning a romantic evening by the fire. ("Honey, are you *sure* this is *Sleepless in Seattle?*")

Imagine the trauma to the kiddies when the baby-sitter slips in what she thinks is a Muppet Babies tape, pats them on the head, and goes downstairs to make lunch.

Right now, while you're thinking of it, inform everyone in your life that should you so much as *think* you see a camera in that delivery room, you will hunt them down one by one and, with painstaking, excruciating slowness, pluck each hair from their heads, one at a time.

10
Rules for a Safe Pregnancy

Nine Months of Paranoia

WHAT YOU DON'T KNOW CAN MAKE YOU CRAZY

"Having a baby has never been safer!" chirp the Experts . . . just before they launch into a grim recitation of the 19,492 incredibly risky things that you, as a *responsible* mother-to-be, must avoid at all costs—*or else* suffer the enormous, tragic, horrifying consequences too tragic and horrifying to enumerate. (Suffice it to say, they are pretty tragic and horrifying.)

Oh, and try to avoid stress, dear. That hurts the baby too.

In book after book, pamphlet after pamphlet, you are urged to be ever-vigilant, on watch, and in a constant state of alert for Danger. If (and only if) you follow The Rules, you might (just might) make it through your pregnancy without doing something incredibly stupid.

You might expect that these Rules for a Safe Pregnancy would stay constant, having been formulated on the basis of some Actual Expertise possessed by

113

some Actual Expert. In fact, no one knows where these pronouncements come from. The source for many of these Rules remains as shrouded in mystery as the origin of those bugs that show up in airtight, hermetically sealed flour canisters.

The Rules for a Safe Pregnancy change from season to season, much like hemlines. Consequently there's no real agreement on anything . . . except that floor-length gowns are inappropriate before dusk.

Do not overeat. Do not undereat. Gain no more than twenty pounds. Gain as much as you want. Do not wear constricting clothes. Wear a sturdy underwire support bra and support hose. Exercise. Take naps. (What are you doing lying down? Didn't we just tell you to exercise??)

To the layperson unschooled in the complexities of Offering Expert Advice and Making Up Rules, these may seem like contradictions. However, they are not. They merely illustrate the rapid vast strides made by science and medicine and agencies run by individuals who become disoriented and confused when they stride rapidly. Consequently, they can't remember what they had for lunch, much less recall what sage scientific doctrine they uttered last week.

Sometimes their mixed messages are merely Official Updated Advice Based on the Results of New Studies. (New Studies are conducted, on average, every four days.) The Experts, you see, must continue to come up with New Improved Rules to which only they are privy. Because if they don't keep changing the rules, eventually everything will be common knowledge and everyone will be as informed as the Experts. BAM! The Experts become obsolete. So it's a daily battle for survival of the specious.

The Experts are, however, running out of things to declare dangerous. So they are now going back and *reassessing* (a scientific and political term meaning "changing one's mind"). Reassessing allows them to declare previously dangerous things A-OK (in moderation, with reservations, and under a doctor's supervision, you understand). After a few years of this they then have a whole new crop of things they can go into a panic over, reassess, and issue urgent warnings and emergency updates on.

Coincidentally, this also results in the necessity of reprinting new updated editions of existing pregnancy manuals. Wouldn't want outdated info being passed around! The author can then announce (with a modest blush) that his recent scholarly, definitive work on pregnancy, *The Definitive Scholarly Guide to Pregnancy*, published two years ago, is now in its twenty-eighth printing.

(As you read this chapter, four more items will be added to the Official List of Dangers and Precautions, three will be deleted, six more will be in the process of being reassessed, and an additional four turned over for debate on "Donahue" and "Oprah.")

BE AFRAID . . . BE VERY AFRAID

You realize, of course, how very fortunate you are to be having your baby now instead of during the Dark

Ages, when nothing was sterile except, of course, men who wore their codpieces too tight.

Everything was dangerous then. Of course, everything is *still* dangerous today. But at least the precautions we employ against modern dangers do not require a working knowledge of the obstetrical uses of chicken entrails and osprey talons.

As recently as the 1950s, or even last week, women walked about just as cheerful as you please, blithely gestating without a care in the world, humming little pregnant-tunes—(quote) *dum-de-deedly-dum-de-dum*—as if everything was peachy keen and nothing was going to happen. All that was required for a happy, safe pregnancy was an array of smock tops and the ability to knit booties. (For further information, consult reruns of "I Love Lucy" episodes, circa 1952.)

It's a miracle any of us is alive. Doctors used to tell women to drink beer to help build their milk supplies. (Here's to good babies—tonight is kind of special.) Valium or a glass of wine was prescribed for "nerves." It's a wonder our mothers weren't advised to include in their daily diets at least six hot dogs, two sticks of margarine, a tub of movie popcorn, and one serving of fish found floating belly up in Boston Harbor. (Some women were, in fact, counseled to do this. Their children now write humor books.)

Considering the ignorant manner in which our mothers had babies just a few decades ago, you'd think we'd all have at least one extra eye or a toe protruding from our foreheads. But, thankfully, most of us don't, and in any case, bangs are in style.

THE TOP TEN THINGS TO OBSESS OVER

1. TOXOPLASMOSIS

Danger! Danger! Do not play with cat poop! This means YOU!

Women who must be warned not to mess around with cat poop should really not be having children at all.

Be that as it may, all pregnancy manuals are required by law to carry dire warnings regarding toxoplasmosis. This is a nasty illness caused by disgusting microscopic creatures with the appropriately disgusting-sounding name *protozoa*.

Now, there are a lot of different kinds of protozoa, and they all look pretty much the same. This is due to the fact that they're single-celled organisms, which, as you might imagine, doesn't leave a whole lot of room for varying personalities and facial features. Because it's hard to distinguish who's who, it's best to walk big wide circles around all protozoa during pregnancy.

The toxoplasmosis variety of protozoa hang out in unsavory places like cat feces. Consequently, these protozoa will make you and the baby very very sick, as is so often the case with items you might encounter when poking about in animal excrement.

So you can see why all the pregnancy manuals are very clear on this matter—Don't be messing with cat poop when you're pregnant.

(It is unclear why cat poop is singled out for warning. One would think that avoiding the feces of all animals would be just an all-around everyday good-hygiene rule of thumb. Apparently owl droppings and wildebeest dung are OK.)

The attractive nature of cat feces is a temptation to be sure, but for the next nine months, do try to avoid the natural impulse to engage in activities that involve feline deposits. You may have to rearrange your schedule for a while, but once the baby is born you may resume normal cat poop frivolities.

2. DRINKING

You will definitely want to refrain from so much as even a drop of alcohol, because if you *do* have a drink, and the baby turns out to look like a marmoset, you will be blamed.

In years past, baby's fussy temperament was attributed to colic, and his eggplant-shaped head was chalked up to Uncle Claude's recessive genes. Now, however, we know that such things are your fault— you and your shameful consorts, Ernest & Julio.

In fact your one glass of wine will be suspected as the root cause for anything and everything that isn't totally and completely perfect. It will be *your fault* if the baby cries. It will be *your fault* if the baby spits up. And when baby is fifteen, giving you that sullen look and muttering things under his breath, it will not be adolescent hormones to blame—oh, no—it's the rum sauce you spooned over the baked pears in your second trimester.

So you must act immediately. Get ruthless. Go through your cupboards—quickly, quickly now! No time to waste! Pour all the vanilla extract down the drain. Gather up all the beer nuts and burn them. Toss out Aunt Fanny's Christmas fruitcake. (Actually, this is a good idea even if you're not pregnant.)

Do not use Scotch tape. Do not play gin rummy. Do not do the rumba or the beer barrel polka. Cover your ears if the radio plays "Sherry" or "Tequila Monday."

If your dog's name is Brandy, shoot it.

3. SMOKING

Do not, under any circumstances, smoke while you're pregnant. The dangers cannot be overstated. The instant you light up, a horde of wild-eyed banshees with six-inch fingernails will hurl themselves at you from out of nowhere, screeching obscenities. (This may well happen even if you're not pregnant. You are in double double extra danger if you happen to be wearing a fur at the same time.)

Don't even sit in the smoking section of a restaurant. The secondhand smoke will waft over to you, get into your lungs, and travel down to the fetus. Your baby will then be born with cigarette breath, which messes up the whole bonding experience. ("Eeeuuuw! Get it outta here! It smells like Cousin LeRoy's car.")

4. CAFFEINE

Research on the effects of caffeine during pregnancy is far from complete, due to the fact that the researchers take so many coffee breaks.

Nevertheless, it is recommended that you stay away from caffeine-containing food and drink—coffee, tea, colas, chocolate; you know, all those things that make life worth living. Instead, replace these empty, malevolent calories in your diet with something wholesome, such as beets. You will hardly notice the difference.

Caffeine, you see, can make you jittery and highstrung. So everyone recommends that you abstain from it throughout your pregnancy—especially your obstetrician, who does not relish your jitteriness and high-strung behavior occurring in his office.

Of course, they neglect to tell you that *abstaining* from caffeine can cause the very same symptoms you seek to avoid—along with headaches, constipation, and the emergence of an intolerable personality, which they will blame on hormones. However, these withdrawal symptoms will eventually diminish in, oh, about nine months, and people will slowly resume attempts at conversation with you—tentatively at first, but with increasing boldness as they see you no longer seek to rip the flesh from their face.

Caffeine also keeps you up at night. Caffeine, you see, is a suspected factor in low-birth-weight babies, and these babies, in their efforts to catch up, will want to feed with the frequency of hummingbirds and will wake you every thirty minutes. However, if you are in your second trimester and the baby already weighs fourteen pounds, run—do not walk—to the nearest espresso bar as fast as your swollen little ankles will carry you. Glare at anyone who dares comment (and there *will* be someone) that, last she heard, pregnant women couldn't *have* coffee.

If you find yourself sneaking away to snort lines of Sanka crystals, help is available. You might want to check into a detoxification facility, such as the Juan Valdez Center.

5. MEDICATIONS

Here's a real catch-22. It is not good for your developing baby when you don't feel well, but you're not allowed to take anything to make you feel better. See, everything that would make *you* feel better makes your *baby* feel like a laboratory rat being force-fed by Kurt Cobain.

Because of your interconnected bloodstreams and digestive systems, medicine taken in amounts suitable for you are way too much for baby. From baby's point of view, the aspirin you take for your headache looks to be an asteroid hurtling its way toward its head.

And the antihistamine you take for your runny nose will cause you to give birth to a shriveled little dehydrated morsel such as you might find in some hiker's knapsack. ("Congratulations, Mrs. Philpot. It's a raisin.")

So for the love of Mike, woman, stay away from the medicine chest. Treat your symptoms naturally, using home remedies such as chicken soup and hot toddies. Of course, the chicken soup must not contain monosodium glutamate, artificial flavors or colors, excess salt, or fat, and the hot toddies must not contain alcohol or sugar or saccharine or aspartame or any herbs with multisyllabic names.

You will get a headache just thinking about it.

6. SEX

There is no consensus among Experts on whether or not it is advisable to continue sexual activity while pregnant. This is because the researchers who get to study this stuff kinda like studying this stuff and would very much like to continue.

If they came up with a decision on the matter, they might be pulled off the good stuff and reassigned to cat poop research. Lingering questions and doubts also mean continued grant money and more really really fun lab experiments.

There does, however, seem to be universal agreement that a woman should not engage in sexual intercourse after her water has broken. Of course, researchers are just guessing about this, since there is no known case of any woman who, upon having just expelled a warm water balloon onto the grocery store floor, turned to the nearest male and demanded, "Take me now, you hunka hunka burnin' love."

7. HOUSEHOLD CHEMICALS

The very name should send shudders down your spine. *Chemicals.* Mysterious substances formulated in shadowy laboratories beneath the earth, bubbling over in test tubes and beakers, spilling onto philodendrons that then mutate into specimens suitable for showing in *The Little Shop of Horrors*.

Even a mere whiff of Pine Sol may be tempting fate. Do you *want* to risk bearing a child who drops needles all over the house? Oh, sure, he'd be handy at Christmastime, but . . .

Actually, of all the Rules for a Safe Pregnancy, avoiding household chemicals is the best one. Since most household chemicals tend to gather in bottles of cleaning products, avoiding such chemicals means that *you won't be cleaning*!

Researchers have assembled no conclusive evidence that *all* household cleaner fumes pose danger. However, in this case, erring on the side of caution seems to be the wisest course, wouldn't you say? Yes, indeedy. There have to be *some* perks to pregnancy. Not having to swish around in the toilet bowl for nine months is one of them.

Of course, it is important that your household be clean and germ-free to provide a healthy, safe environment for you and your baby. Sooooooo . . . everyone else will have to clean for you. Make sure every member of your family knows about this! Call meetings. Post notices.

If they seem to be getting lax, drag out a bottle of ammonia, a bucket, and a mop. Head for the bathroom. Sigh heavily. Then smile bravely at your older children, saying in a tremulous little voice, "Promise me you won't make fun of your little brother if he has antlers."

Unfortunately, staying away from household

chemicals is not entirely without a downside. Hair coloring falls under the heading of household chemicals as well, and experts caution women to refrain from using these products during pregnancy. Evidently these chemicals can seep through your scalp, cross the placental barrier, and turn your baby into a floozy with dry, overprocessed split ends.

Abstaining from hair color also allows passersby to gauge the progress of your pregnancy. ("Ooooh . . . your roots are at four and a half inches now, dearie—you could go into labor any day! I went to five inches, myself, but it was a difficult pregnancy.")

8. PESTICIDES

The danger of pesticides was graphically illustrated in the 1959 movie *North By Northwest,* in which Cary Grant was chased down by a crop duster. Though he was not pregnant at the time, it should be noted that he did eventually die—as did the film's director, Alfred Hitchcock, who, although he spent much of his life sporting a third-trimester belly, never *did* deliver that child.

Chilling as that is, you are probably thinking that since you are not being sprayed by a crop duster on a regular basis, you're safe. Well, what about all those lawn services and exterminators plying their trade about your neighborhood? You think they've got club soda in those canisters? If it's not good for grub worms, it won't be good for baby.

Your best bet is to invest in a good army-surplus gas mask. The mere sight of a pregnant woman waddling out in chemical warfare gear flailing her arms and pointing to the sky will send them packing.

And, of course, you must consider the foods you eat. Were they sprayed with dangerous pesticides? (If you live in a country with indoor plumbing, the answer is yes.)

You *could* spend hours at the sink scrubbing all your food, but then standing for any length of time will make your ankles swell up like enormous, insect-infested rutabagas.

Or you could grow your own veggies. Of course, this involves unpleasant agriculture-related activities such as bending and hand-picking garden slugs off the lettuce.

Better switch to just buying organically grown foods. You can distinguish them from their sprayed counterparts in the supermarket by looking for the exorbitant price tag and enormous worm-holes.

Bon appétit.

9. AIR POLLUTANTS

What you breathe baby breathes. But because baby is so tiny, the effect is magnified a hundred times over— meaning that baby has probably deduced that it has had the misfortune of implanting itself into a uterus located on the tailpipe of a Greyhound bus.

Because of the volume of noxious gases and filthy particles that float about in the air, you might conclude that it would be a good idea to avoid breathing altogether during pregnancy. Get this out of your head. Women who breathe throughout their pregnancies have, on average, far fewer complications than those who do not.

So instead of holding your breath for nine months, it's best to try to minimize your exposure to air pollutants, such as those emitted by cars and trucks, factories, tire fires, volcanoes, and all patrons of White Castle and Taco Bell.

You could move to an unspoiled island paradise. (Be sure to select an island far removed from volcanoes and whose indigenous people are not in the habit of eating the tourists.) The simplest solution, though, is merely to file a report with the Environmental Protection Agency and the National Wildlife Service, informing them that there is an albino Crested Kangaroo Rat living in your shrubs. Federal bureaucrats will immediately issue a flurry of court orders and directives sealing off your neighborhood, prohibiting all emissions within a fifty-mile radius, and arresting all patrons of Taco Bell.

10. ENVIRONMENTAL DANGERS: MAGNETIC FIELDS, RADIATION, RADON, ASBESTOS

All of these hazards fall under the jurisdiction of the government and are subject to its laws, regulations, and statutes. Consequently you will not be able to make sense of any of it.

If you are wondering whether or not the area in which you live harbors these dangers, look out the window. Do you see cars? Lights? Streets? If so, the answer is yes. Environmental dangers abound in areas served by modern technology, which includes everywhere, with the possible exception of rural areas of Nepal and Mississippi.

And even if you are lucky enough to live in one of those nontechnological areas, you are still at risk for radon, which occurs naturally wherever there is soil. Consequently, the only place safe from radon is downtown Manhattan. Unfortunately, the safety benefit of New York's no-soil environment is canceled out by crazed taxi drivers and Howard Stern.

Asbestos, too, is everywhere. That's because decades ago the government said that asbestos was a Good Thing and wrote laws forcing all of us to stuff our buildings with it. (Not surprisingly, this took place at about the same time the government suggested that in the event of a nuclear attack you should "turn off stove burners and hide under a table or a desk.")

Now, however, we know that asbestos is a Bad Thing. Of course, that does not mean that government officals were wrong when they said asbestos was a Good Thing. It just means they were morons.

When it comes to radiation, things have come full circle. The government used to downplay the risks to prevent panic. In the sixties, these officials assured us that pregnant women and schoolchildren could survive an atom bomb hit in the neighborhood if they merely followed Civil Defense guidelines to "look away" from the mushroom cloud and cover their heads with their arms until they received the all-clear sign.

Now, however, we know a lot more about the government's role in radiation, if not about radiation itself. The recent discovery of heretofore unknown pages from the original Constitution (found in Dan Rostenkowski's basement) show clearly that the Founding Fathers believed that the role of government is not to prevent panic but to instigate it. That's why we are now being issued warnings about *everything*.

However, thanks to public service announcements such as *Silkwood* and *The China Syndrome*, most of the populace is aware that it's best for people to avoid radiation. Pregnant women are pretty much informed about this too, and unless they have a deep, abiding desire to give birth to a squid, they routinely "just say no" to the recreational use of plutonium and x-rays.

But that is not enough for the Experts. They want you to fear the possible hazards of Everything, including things *you cannot avoid or do anything about.* So now you must worry about microwaves, TVs, VCRs, computers, high-tension wires, power tools, cellular phones, video games, hair dryers, toasters, digital clocks—basically, everything that distinguishes your household from the ones depicted on "Little House on the Prairie."

Since eliminating all modern conveniences from your life is probably impossible, the least you can do is attempt to minimize them. Vacation in Amish communities. Move to Bora Bora. Stay at a Motel 6.

11

And Just in Case You Have No Common Sense . . .

Safety Tips for Clueless Preggos

The bulk of the advice proffered on safety in the many conventional books and pamphlets on pregnancy will strike you as being rather . . . um . . . *obvious*. In fact, some of the advice may insult your intelligence. (If it does not, take it as a warning sign that you are a dangerously incompetent twit who has no business procreating. May I interest you in some Norplant today?)

If you are a normal, reasonably intelligent human being, a look of perplexed incredulity should creep across your face when reading earth-shattering revelations such as this: "Pregnant women should avoid walking on icy slopes in spike-heeled pumps."

You will be sternly cautioned to watch your step on steep staircases; to stay off ladders; to fasten your seat belt; to be careful when walking on wet, slick floors; to avoid contact sports; to avoid lifting extremely heavy items; to refrain from drinking contaminated water; to stay away from sick people; etc., etc., etc.

After reading through all this, your natural response will be to snort something to the effect of "Well, DUH!"

So why do they put in all those stupid, obvious safety tips that seem to be written in the same tone of voice used by Mr. Rogers when counseling Mr. McFeely on the proper way to hang up a sweater?

There are two possible explanations. One, the givers of advice are convinced you have the common sense of Velveeta; or two, they have run out of useful things to say and need to fill up the rest of the book. Clearly the answer is both one and two.

OBVIOUS DANGERS NO ONE HAS THOUGHT TO POINT OUT TO YOU BEFORE

Since so many of the safety warnings issued to pregnant moms are an exercise in the obvious ("Avoid cliff diving in your ninth month") it's curious why the Experts neglect so many *other* obvious safety hazards. Where are the admonitions against the following behaviors?

• poking forks into electrical outlets
• sticking your tongue on icy windows
• picking up hitchhikers
• sticking your leg into a wood chipper

The same people who deem it necessary to caution pregnant women against rummaging about in cat poop have somehow overlooked the really important obvious things to avoid. This borders on criminal neglect. How could any responsible publisher omit a warning to pregnant women about the dangers of placing a cup of scorching hot coffee between their legs in a fast-food drive-through?

And where are the cautionary notes regarding putting one's hand in the garbage disposal?

And it's not just one—*each* and *every* book out today FAILS to alert you to these dangers:

STAY AWAY FROM . . .

- *DOWNED POWER LINES.* Electrocution often means trouble for pregnant moms! If you see a sparking, spitting electrical wire writhing about the ground, WALK AWAY!

- *EXPLOSIVES.* Be especially conscientious about washing your hands after handling any incendiary devices or other explosive material. If you are a member of a terrorist organization where this is an occupational hazard, you might ask to be transferred to a less risky assignment, such as spokesperson in charge of placing the phone call to the media to take credit for a bombing.

- *CARNIVOROUS ANIMALS.* Just to be on the safe side, pregnant women should avoid encounters with grizzly bears, lions, crocodiles, and piranha, which may mistake you for a steamship round of beef.

- *NATURAL DISASTERS.* Tornadoes, hurricanes, earthquakes, floods, volcanic eruptions, and forest fires are all off limits to you, young lady! Network newspeople will, of course, encourage you to have your baby during one of these occurrences, but DO NOT LISTEN TO THEM.

OTHER THINGS TO AVOID:

- automatic weapons
- sulphuric acid
- arsenic
- broken glass
- spoiled pork
- killer bees
- satanic cults
- severed arteries
- lightning
- cholera
- malfunctioning carnival rides
- rabid bats
- Bosnia
- faulty brakes
- sputum of unknown origin
- Spam

And of course, now's the time to review all those safety tips you learned as a child. Heeding the admonishments of your parents and grandparents is even more vital now than it was then:

- Don't eat the apple core. A tree will grow in your stomach, and you'll have branches growing out of your ears.

- Don't run with a lollipop in your mouth.
- Don't swallow your gum. It sticks to your insides and clogs things up until eventually you die.
- If you make a face, someday it's just going to freeze like that.
- Put down that stick before you put someone's eye out.

THE REALLY USEFUL STUFF NO ONE TELLS YOU

So, OK . . . now you know all the basic safety tips that you could have deduced on your own—assuming, of course, that you are over the age of five. But what about the REAL dangers that present themselves only to pregnant women? Because of your new body, things that used to be safe are no longer safe. Consequently, you should observe the following:

- DO NOT IRON IN THE NUDE. Your new enlarged belly and new improved breasts make this a risky business. In the past, while ironing *au naturel*, your body parts pretty much stayed up and off the ironing board. Now, however, your breasts will flop themselves into the path of the oncoming iron. Aside from the intolerable pain, breasts, as a rule, look better without scorch marks and a crisp crease.

- DO NOT RIDE ON ESCALATORS. Getting off an escalator requires precision timing. You must coordinate the position of your feet with the disappearing last step. This, of course, requires that you actually be able to see your feet, which you cannot. You will then fall headlong into a display of imported crystal stemware and owe the store $7,000.

- DO NOT SWIM IN UNFAMILIAR WATERS. While this safety tip shows up in many standard Red Cross swimming pamphlets, its importance to expectant mothers is often underestimated. The pregnant woman, you see, bears a striking resemblance to any of a number of tasty marine mammals such as you might find off the coast of Alaska or on the Discovery channel. On a cloudy day an inattentive killer whale could easily mistake you for a sea lion.

- DO NOT USE THE REST ROOM ON AN AIRPLANE. Once you have wedged yourself into the tiny little cubicle, you will not be able to get out. Furthermore, you won't even be able to *use* the facilities, since there is no room in which to maneuver and you will be unable to take down your pants. The sign will blink and beep at you, ordering you to return to your seat—which you would gladly do if your stomach weren't lodged in the sink. After an emergency landing, a rescue team will extract you with the Jaws of Life as camera crews capture the whole event, including the part where you wet your pants, for airing on next week's episode of "Rescue 911."

12
Childbirth Class

Training a Skilled Labor Force

Humans, the highest order of mammal and the only species currently allowed to sign contracts and hold public office, are the only life form seemingly dumbfounded as to how to give birth to their young.

People who are regularly entrusted with one another's finances and allowed to propel two-ton motor vehicles through a residential area are presumed to be clueless in matters of childbirth. Without training classes and mountains of books, humans would flounder about, muddling their way through the whole experience.

PREGNANT WOMAN:	"I think what I'll do is carry this baby for oh, about twelve weeks, tops."
MAN:	"If you want, I'll take a shift on weekends."
WOMAN:	"OK. Let's play it by ear."

135

Without guidance, they'd never figure out how to let nature take its course.

Here's a typical expectant couple now. Let's listen in:

PREGNANT WOMAN: (looking down at belly with perplexed expression)	"I just can't seem to figure out how I'm going to get this person out of here."
MAN: (concerned)	"Well, you better think of something soon. It's getting bigger."
WOMAN:	"I know. I might have waited too long already. I think it's too big to pull up through my ear now."
MAN: (taking measurements of wife's ear)	"Most of the obvious exit routes *are* starting to look inadequate. Maybe you have a design flaw?"
WOMAN: (She begins a search of her body.)	"Yeah. You'd think there'd be a bigger opening here somewhere."
MAN:	"Maybe you could ask Myra. She had a baby inside of her once, and she got it out."
WOMAN: (shaking head vehemently)	"Are you crazy? You wouldn't *believe* the preposterous story she tells about how she got it out. The woman needs help."

MAN: "Well, how 'bout we tie the
(looking hopeful)   umbilical cord to the trailer
                        hitch on the Blazer? Couple
                        of good revs oughta do it."

WOMAN: "No, let's just boil water
                        and call a cab."

Fortunately, we now have childbirth classes, which have made enormous progress in establishing an approved, consistent plan of action—so important to today's busy woman. ("Winging it" is not an Approved Childbirth Method.)

Even if you have given birth before, you will be required to go to school again. Science, as we have noted previously, continues progress at break-neck speed, with almost daily revelations that render any previous childbirth experience dangerously obsolete. You would not want to jeopardize the success of the proceedings by breathing in an unscientific manner. ("For the love of God, Mrs. Lipschultz! What do you think you're *DOING*?! Have you lost your *MIND*?")

If you do not graduate from an accredited Professional School of Childbirth, they will act as if you are not permitted to give birth. They take a dim view of dropouts. "Sorry, but without a diploma we simply cannot allow you to have that child. You should have stayed in school."

Well, then. That's that. You certainly don't want to have to carry your child until you are the size of Greenland, now do you?

Unfortunately, there are no correspondence classes offering registration via matchbook covers.

("Become a certified aircraft mechanic or childbearer at home!")

There are no full-page ads at the back of crossword puzzle books for the Home Study Institute of Birthing, urging you to send for the easy aptitude test. ("If you can push this block through that round hole, you may have what it takes to be a mom!")

So you might as well resign yourself to attending class. But first you need a coach.

VINCE LOMBARDI MEETS BUTTERFLY MCQUEEN

The idea for childbirth coaches originated with obstetricians, midwives, and nurses who got tired of women in labor yelling at them. It was far better, they decided, to have mothers yelling at *someone else*—ideally, the father of the child. Not surprisingly, when expectant fathers were first approached with this idea, they declined the opportunity to sit silently for up to thirty-two hours while a sweating, grunting woman screamed obscenities at them. "No thanks," they said. "We'd rather have red ants crawling over our genitals."

Women, however, liked this idea and sent it to a marketing firm to repackage it for greater appeal. By simply relabeling the idea with a masculine-sounding name, the idea caught on.

"Hey, how'd you like to be your wife's *coach*?"

"You mean like Mike Ditka or John Madden?"

"Yeah, something like that."

"Sure!"

So, your partner will be all enthused about this. Taking seriously his position of authority and responsibility, he'll step up his ESPN time ("Research, hon!"), wear a whistle, and schedule practice drills. ("I've clocked driving time to the hospital. Knocked 3.5 seconds off my best time.")

He may even post motivational posters around the house (JUST DO IT) and attempt to inspire you with encouraging slogans:

- "No pain, no gain."
- "When the going gets tough, the tough get going."
- "Get out there and win one for the Gipper."
- "I wanna see a lean, mean baby machine!"

Once he is firmly committed to acting as your coach, his friends who have already done this will fill him in on what a childbirth coach really does. They'll explain that, no, he can't yell and cuss and swear and throw chairs. That is the *mother's* role.

His role is to be supportive and encouraging—which means exactly what the *woman* says it means at any given moment. ("Massage my back. Don't touch me! Get the %$% away from me! Just where do you think *you're* going? Get back here and massage my back!")

His role is to take whatever you dish out.

WOMAN: "URRRRRUNGGGHH."

MAN: "You're doing great!"

WOMAN: "*YOU* DID THIS TO ME!!!
              PIG!! SLIME!"

MAN: "That's my girl!"

WOMAN: "SUCK AN EGG.
            RRRRRAARRGHNNGH."
MAN: "Just relax and B-R-E-A-T-H-E."
WOMAN: "EAT DIRT AND *DIE!*"
MAN: "You're doing great. Just great."

Now that you've got that squared away, you can begin class.

PREGGO HALL:
AN ACADEMY FOR YOUNG WOMEN

All childbirth institutes of higher learning operate under the presumption that you are an incompetent twit. Worse, you are a layperson, an *amateur*.

And, of course, it is dangerous and irresponsible to let untrained amateurs give birth since it involves highly scientific endeavors such as grunting and breathing and words such as *PUSH* and *aaaaarrrggh*.

Left to their own devices, women would undoubtedly engage in all manner of unscientific, unproved childbirth methods, such as attempting to cough it up. ("No, Mrs. Kravinski, you *cannot* induce labor with Robitussin.")

So you must be taught one of the Official, Approved Methods of Childbirth. Classes are all based on pretty much the same curriculum, which involves instruction in the art of relaxation and breathing—the same basic course material found in martial arts classes. (In fact there are childbirth classes taught by sensei at the Tai Kwondo Academy where, in addition to breathing, you'll practice blood-curdling screams and become proficient in head-to-cervix combat.)

You will be schooled in the discipline of Lamaze, Read, Bradley, or, most likely, some sort of hybrid of all three. This provides effective camouflage for the instructor to sneak in little changes and alterations for her own amusement. ("Remember now, moms, you'll be focusing and breathing, focusing and breathing, except for every third contraction, when you'll be squeezing your left breast and yodeling.")

YOUR CLASSMATES

You will join with about ten other couples, carefully selected by the instructor for their incompatibility with any other class participants—all of whom will be persons who, if they moved into your neighborhood, would prompt an immediate call to your own realtor.

Each class must be represented by the following couples:

Mr. & Mrs. Earnest Intensity

This couple takes notes, tape-records each meeting, knows the answer to each and every question, and brandishes Olympic-caliber stopwatches. ("With a contraction lasting 45.432144 seconds, your cleansing breath needs to be 3.1491 seconds longer, sugar-lump.") They arrive early and stay late, engaging in theoretic discussions until the janitor threatens to lock them in. By the last class, even the instructor is clenching her teeth.

Mr. & Mrs. Potato Head

These people are one fry short of a Happy Meal. They don't understand anything that's going on and are, in fact, not at all certain just what they're doing there. Classmates' concern grows with each of their rare utterances. ("We had a cat what had a litter one time 'neath the stairwell. Pa took 'em out to the barn, and we never did see 'em again.")

Mr. & Mrs. Dewey Hafftu

Clearly, they'd rather be *anywhere* else. Recognizable by their rolling eyeballs and loud sighs, this couple is royally miffed to be missing the night's episodes of "Cops" and "Hard Copy." Sulking and slouching, they use this time to clean their fingernails and take inventory of their wallets.

Mr. & Mrs. Ben Theredunnthat

This couple will, at every opportunity, *correct* the instructor's information based on the actual experiences they've gone through, which they gleefully chronicle in excruciating, boring detail. First-time parents' questions or comments are met with condescending snickers. By the fourth class someone will jump them both from behind with the demonstration polyvinyl umbilical cord.

Mr. & Mrs. Howie Dewin

Eager, enthusiastic, and nauseatingly cheerful. ("Is this right? Like this? C'mere, c'mere, watch this.")

They dress in matching outfits and have mounted and matted prints of their ultrasounds as mementos for each of their classmates.

Mr. & Mrs. Frank Lee Horrified

This couple will become offended and/or embarrassed by absolutely everything. When the plastic uterus is passed to them, they'll recoil as if they'd been offered a soiled diaper. When films of an actual birth are shown, they'll leave in a huff, informing the instructor that under no circumstances will they have any part in such filth. *They* are not *those* kind of people.

OK, STUDENTS, PAY ATTENTION

You will be expected to come to class properly prepared with your materials, which include mats and pillows such as you might bring to day care. Many couples (notably those arriving in Volvos) will have attractive, specially designed preggo mats and pillows with matching covers. ("We picked them up at a little boutique in the Hamptons. Only $245!")

You, however, will waddle in bearing your neighbor child's Dream Barbie Slumber Party Bag, feeling like an overgrown kindergartener on the first day of school, heartbroken at having forgotten your Barbie lunchbox and thermos to go with the rest of your ensemble.

Your instructor, who will have taken speech training at Kindercare ("Mommies, daddies, everybody on their mats, now!"), will first go around the room and make each participant tell something about

herself. At the end of the first class you will be
intimately familiar with your classmates' educational backgrounds, genealogy, unreliable birth control experiences, and/or recent major appliance
purchases.

This information will, of course, be incredibly
useful to you during childbirth. ("AAAARHHGGH!"
"You're doing great, honey, just great. Way to push!
Just keep thinking about DeeDee and Dexter's new
Chevy S-10 pickup!")

ANATOMY 101

You will be shown slides on an overhead projector
that purport to represent the female reproductive system. The diagrams, however, clearly illustrate the
head of an ancient Egyptian goat god.

As the slides advance, you'll learn that the uterus
is, in fact, an enormous lima bean. Further diagrams—allegedly depicting the external parts of the
female—appear to chart the solar system. ("As you
can see, Neptune has two moons. . . .")

During one of the classes your instructor will
drag out a prop box suspiciously similar to those
found in the basements of psychotic serial killers.
Rummaging through the life-size plastic body parts,
she will seize the reproductive-oriented ones and pass
them around as party favors.

The highlight of the evening is the plastic uterus,
which you are expected to examine and inspect and
turn over and admire like a particularly well-formed
conch shell washed in by the tide. Resist the impulse

to hold it up to your ear—"Why, I can hear the ocean!"

Your classmates will either toss it off like a hot potato or make smart-aleck comments. ("Uterus, huh? Looks to me like an avocado. Guacamole, anyone? Ahhahaha!")

The *proper* etiquette when handed a uterus by a complete stranger is to avoid eye contact, then nod and raise your eyebrows with great interest as you rotate it to get a good look at every angle— "Hmmmhmmm. Ah-ha. Fascinating"—after which you quickly hand it off to the next person and scurry off to the bathroom to wash your hands.

You will be given a tour of the hospital and its state-of-the-art maternity wing, where you will see the neonatal unit with its rows of beautiful babies swaddled up snugly in pink and blue blankets. (Every so often you'll see one that looks like a fully cooked Cornish hen. Do not be alarmed. In an effort to cut costs and consolidate services, hospitals make use of vacant incubators as warming ovens for meal service to the rest of the hospital.)

You will be shown pleasantly decorated, homey-looking labor rooms, where calm, serene, beautifully reposing women lay propped in bed, calmly and efficiently dilating as their handsome, empathetic husbands gently stroke their foreheads, exchanging warm, tender smiles.

Of course, these are actors. The *real* labor rooms are located behind soundproof steel barriers, containing *real* women in labor whose husbands are, at this moment, deftly dodging flying bedpans.

RELAXATION AND THE
LOST ART OF BREATHING

As described in the chapter on the various methods of childbirth, relaxation is the key to an effortless birth. What could be simpler?

Merely lie back and let the cares and stress of the day just melt away while you float along on imaginary waves . . . you're relaxed, limp . . . the sun bathing you in its warmth . . . caressed by gentle tropical breezes . . . A GREAT WHITE SHARK CLAMPS HIS JAWS ABOUT YOUR MIDSECTION . . . you ignore him . . . drifting along . . . breathing . . . the sun bathing you in its warmth . . .

See how easy this is?

Well, OK, it does take practice. But that's what you're there for, right? To do this, you and your classmates will spread out about the room and lie down on your mats, creating the overall visual impression of a field of giant molehills.

The lights will be dimmed, and you will recline comfortably, lulled and soothed by gentle music and sounds and images of water lapping at the seashore, as the instructor's hypnotic singsong voice drones on and on about something or other. ("You're drifting along on an ice floe, an enormous lazy sea cow. . . .")

Of course, achieving relaxation in this setting is somewhat easier than achieving relaxation during labor and delivery, during which your beach scene will resemble something more along the lines of the landing at Normandy, where accompanying the sound of lapping waves will be mortar fire, shrieking seagulls, and moaning casualties.

All the while you'll be instructed to breathe. *In. Out. In. Out.* (Is there any other way? Could you be that set in your ways?) Just to see what happens, you recklessly throw caution to the wind. *Out. In. Out. In.* That's it—live on the edge!

After about a half hour of this, the instructor will go around the room and shake the husbands awake, and the class will continue.

You'll be taught about cleansing breaths and panting and all the accompanying sound effects you must make. *Hee hee hee. Hoo hoo hoo hoo. Wee wee wee wee. Hoo hoo hoo hoo.*

Those passing by will think they've happened upon a wildlife insane asylum or the barnyard version of *Hooked on Phonics.*

Half of the class will hyperventilate and pass out. The other half will go into hysterics and wet their pants.

CONTRACTIONS

You will now learn about contractions. No, not labor pains, you imbecile! Contractions.

Where have you been, girl? Labor pains no longer exist. They were banned in most civilized countries years ago, replaced by the much more modern and comfortable *contraction.*

Contractions, you see, conjure up benign images—tightening, flexing—no more strenuous than a good workout on the ab machine at the gym. How exhilarating!

In fact the word *pain* is absent from the entire proceedings. Your instructor may coyly allude to "discomfort" or "pressure"—as if labor were no more than a bad case of dyspepsia after a large meal. ("Epidural? No thanks, just a couple of Tums oughta do it.")

You are expected to go along with this little charade even if you know better. ("Pressure? You mean like the kind of pressure you get when a fire hose is turned on full force in your ear? Or like an eighteen wheeler backing up on your stomach?")

To point out the facts would spoil it for the others, much as if you were to divulge to wide-eyed preschoolers the résumé of the jolly old man in the mall they thought was Santa Claus who is, in fact, an ex-con with outstanding warrants for child molestation in three states.

In class you will practice contractions by tightening your calf muscles or by having your coach squeeze your arm or toe. ("You know, this would be more realistic if we used pliers.") These simulations parallel actual contractions in the same way bumper cars simulate a demolition derby.

During all of this, you will be FOCUSING. Focusing involves concentrating all of your energies on one spot so as to draw out the pain, where it may then be inflicted on something or someone besides you—as illustrated in childbirth training films such as *Carrie* and *Firestarter*. For this reason you will be instructed to select a noncombustible focal point and to avoid eye contact with hospital personnel.

ADDITIONAL CURRICULUM

When you're not relaxing or contracting or focusing or imitating deranged howler monkeys, you will be given Important Information about the birth process in the form of pamphlets whose illustrations were evidently chosen from the finalists in a competition of fifth-grade art students.

(Unfortunately, anyone who might find these pamphlets informative would not likely possess the skills needed to read them. Nevertheless, you will be handed these illuminating leaflets for the same reason shampoo manufacturers find it necessary to print directions on the bottle. "Wet. Lather. Rinse. Repeat.")

In addition, your instructor will tell you the following things:

- HOW TO RECOGNIZE THE ONSET OF LABOR. First, there's the dislodging of the mucous plug— known by the attractive name "bloody show"— which, for the last nine months, has kept baby from crawling out in the middle of the night and scaring the bejeebies out of you. ("What the . . . ??!")

  But not to worry. Like a bug in a champagne bottle, baby stays trapped until the cork pops. Then it's party time.

  Next, the amniotic sac will rupture. Called the "breaking of waters," this will almost always occur while you are standing in line at a checkout counter or sitting on a white brocade couch in a furniture showroom.

  For this reason many women carry a jar of pickles or a sixteen-ounce cup of Mountain Dew in their purses as a diversionary device. ("OOPS! Look what you made me do.")

- HOW AND WHEN TO PUSH. First and foremost, you must never ever push unless you've been given permission. Your body, unfortunately, doesn't give a flying fig about *what* Simon Says—and will go into push mode when it darn well feels like it. So people will be shouting orders at you. "DO NOT PUSH! YOU ARE NOT AUTHORIZED TO PUSH! DISENGAGE AND AWAIT CLEARANCE FROM THE CONTROL TOWER." Of course, this is about as effective as telling someone in midair to stop falling.

FEATURE FILM FESTIVAL

Finally, they feel you're ready for the main attraction—a film of an Actual, Live Birth.

Grunting. Sweating. Thrashing. Grimacing. And, ohmigod, *blood*.

Mr. and Mrs. Frank Lee Horrified get up and walk out. The Howie Dewins gasp with delight while Mr. and Mrs. Ben Theredunnthat scoff and guffaw. ("Yeah, right! Like they'd all be so attentive if there weren't cameras.") Mrs. Potato Head whispers to the instructor that she's sure there's been a mistake and she'd just like to forget the whole thing, if that's all right.

You watch this miraculous event—awed, amazed, frightened—trying to absorb its impact, all the while maintaining remarkable control over your gag reflex.

Suddenly, out of nowhere, totally irrelevant thoughts pop into your head—*How much did they PAY this woman to sign a release to have this film shown? (It had to be a LOT.) Lookit that hair. She looks like a demented cockatiel. Jeez, she's got big legs. Wonder how much it would take to get ME to go on film like this? Ten million? Twenty? And who's that woman on the left? Stuff a sock in it, lady!*

The narrator says something about effacement. You think the baby's coming now, but you can't be sure.

Could be a ham. In fact, that's exactly what it looks like. One of those canned hams you can't get out of the tin. (Well, it does.) Here it comes . . . here comes the head. Criminy, she just keeps stretching! Jeez, lady, please don't rip.

Your husband whispers that it looks like an aerial view of Michael Jordan putting on a turtleneck. You smack him on the arm.

The head emerges, then the shoulders. The rest slips out like a flounder, and the mother falls back in elated exhaustion. Someone in the rear of the classroom yells, "Now run it again backwards!"

13

Emotions

Bungee Jumping with Your Psyche

HORMONES

In the Dark Ages anything that could not be explained or understood was chalked up to the supernatural. Spirits. Sorcery. Magic.

Today, however, we are enlightened, educated, and totally scientific. We no longer believe in witches and ghosts and angry spirits. We believe in hormones. Anything we don't understand is blamed on hormones.

Most women have roughly 1.2 bazillion hormones. When a woman becomes pregnant, however, these hormones explode and undergo rapid cell division, reproducing like maniacs at a rate of up to ten thousand times per hour. To give you an idea how fast this is, an adolescent with PMS has hormones that reproduce only six thousand times per hour.

Though you can't see them, you now have literally kajillions of hormones. You're teeming with them. With the aid of electron microscopes and infrared cameras, however, scientists are able to observe these hordes of hormones swarming about your system and to actually see the deranged, maniacal looks on their little faces.

We've already gone through the effects they have on the body. The emotional effects are equally startling, and if you are not aware of what's occurring, you may conclude that you have lost your mind. This is, of course, not the case. You have NOT lost your mind; you've merely gained several thousand more.

Let's describe this in technical terms: basically, hormones hurl themselves like asteroids into your brain, causing your personality to fracture into a billion tiny pieces. Consequently, you now have a wealth of personalities from which to choose on any given day. Change hourly if you want to!

This is Nature's way of ensuring that no woman has to go through her pregnancy alone.

With a cast of thousands occupying the space that once housed just one personality, things can get crowded. There will be lots of pushing and shoving and elbowing, and you can never be quite sure which one will pop to the surface.

Dopey? Happy? Touchy? Weepy? Around and around she goes, and where she stops nobody knows.

The very husband who's walked into the house saying the very same thing for six years ("Hi, honey, I'm home!") will cause you to (select one):

a. burst into tears
b. laugh uncontrollably
c. fly into a rage
d. become incredibly depressed

e. hug and kiss everyone around you

f. eat the entire contents of the fridge

The answer is, of course, "all of the above, depending on what day it is."

And it doesn't have to be anything that's actually said. It could be the way he walks in the door. ("I see you hung up your coat *before* you took off your shoes. Would you like to explain yourself?") It doesn't even have to be your husband. It could be Ted Koppel or Jay Leno. Margaret Thatcher or Oprah Winfrey. It doesn't even have to be a person. A couch could do it. Or a doorknob. Or a spatula.

TOUCHY HORMONES

You can be sitting there, content and relaxed with friends and family, enjoying a pleasant conversation over dinner. Then some insensitive dolt has to spoil it all:

DOLT: "Please pass the breadsticks."

YOU: "Breadsticks? Did you say . . . *breadsticks*?"

DOLT: "Yes. Please pass the breadsticks."

YOU: "BREADSTICKS, huh? What in the HELL is THAT supposed to mean???"

DOLT: (blinking rapidly) "Uh, it means I'd like some breadsticks."

YOU: "I'll just BET you would, buster! If it's not breadsticks, it's something else, isn't it? Oh, *yesssssss*, it's always something. Here, TAKE the stinking, lousy breadsticks. I HOPE YOU CHOKE!"

WEEPY HORMONES

Later that evening. Same dinner. Same people.

DOLT: "Please pass the mashed potatoes."

YOU: "Mashed . . . *potatoes*?"

DOLT: "Yes, please pass the mashed potatoes."

YOU: (lower lip begins to quiver, hands tremble, and tears well in your eyes as you reach for the bowl) "I love mashed potatoes. I always have. Ever since I was a little girl, I loved mashed potatoes. Grandma used to make them from scratch. It's hard to find *good* mashed potatoes anymore, y'know? Just like everything else. Everywhere you go. Not like it used to be. Nothing's like it used to be."

DOLT: "Yeah, well . . ."

YOU: (bursting into tears) "Here, take them, *just take them*, dammit. What do you care?"

SENTIMENTAL HORMONES

Same dinner . . .

DOLT: "Please pass the apple pie."

YOU: "Apple pie! God love ya, isn't that just *perfect*? Here we are, all of us together—friends, family—the way things were *meant* to be. And now, apple pie, God love ya. We are SO blessed."

DOLT: "Yes. Please pass the pie."

YOU: "It's what it's all about, y'know? It's what's *real*. It's about what *matters*—Mom, country,

and apple pie. It's at these times I'm reminded of the words of our founding
fathers . . . (you break into song) Oh, beautiful, for spacious skies, for amber waves of
grain. . . ."

DOLT: "That was Kate Smith."

YOU: (throwing arms around him in warm em-
brace) "Dontcha just *love* this guy?"

Of course, there will also be Depressed Hormones, Giddy Hormones, Elated Hormones, Dramatic
Hormones, and Obsessive Hormones to round out any
dinner party.

YOUR MANY MOODS

As the Experts are fond of pointing out, your hormones are in a constant state of flux throughout pregnancy. (Experts are always using words like *flux*—
which sounds like a combination bleach/fabric soft-
ener—so as to disguise the fact they have no idea
what they're talking about.) *Flux*, in the context of
pregnancy, however, means "endless variety of
moods."

GUERNSEY-HOLSTEIN MOOD

Otherwise known as the "I Feel Like a Cow Mood,"
this mood is a frequent visitor.

Obviously brought on by your enlarged condition,
this state of mind demands constant reassurance
from friends and loved ones that you are still attractive. Their favorite ploy in this endeavor is to tell you

that all pregnant women have a "glow" about them.

Of course, you don't believe this. And even if it were true, you're pretty sure it doesn't apply to you. But they will continue to insist that, yes, yes, it's true—you absolutely GLOW!

Then you start to think about other things that glow—

- *RUDOLPH'S NOSE.* Of course, all the other reindeer laughed and called him names. They wouldn't let poor Rudolph play in any reindeer games.

- *FLEA MARKET ITEMS SOLD FROM THE BACK OF RUSTED STATION WAGONS.* Skull key rings, religious figurines, puff paintings on velvet. Highly attractive, classy items.

- *E.T.'S FOREFINGER.* This glow always preceded the word *Ouuuuuch,* which pretty much parallels the chain of events up to and including childbirth.

While experiencing the Guernsey-Holstein effect, try to avoid situations that will exacerbate the condition, e.g., visiting the petites department of the dress store, cheerleading practice, or Club Med.

Certain television programming is also hard on your tender psyche. Under the best of circumstances, watching the Miss Universe pageant can be a humbling experience. Watching it while you are pregnant is suicidal. (Miss Sweden glides down the runway in her skintight beaded, sequined gown. You observe that, should you be so attired, you would look like the White House Christmas tree.)

There is, however, good alternative programming for this special time in your life. C-SPAN's live coverage of Congress in session is especially helpful if you wish to feel good about your body, since it features, for the most part, people who, if they were nude, would be shot on sight.

The vast array of nature shows on the Discovery channel feature animals with no waistlines. If you're lucky, you can catch the episodes that show obese bears readying themselves for hibernation with huge excesses of fat deposits.

Other programs to make you feel better about your physical appearance:

- "STAR TREK: THE NEXT GENERATION" RERUNS. Should you be feeling self-conscious about your "pregnancy mask," sixty minutes with Lieutenant Worf should make you feel like a new woman. Educational bonus: Position the TV above you, and Captain Jean-Luc Picard's head provides a realistic simulation of "crowning" as reflected in the delivery room mirror.

- "TODAY." Tune in only for the Willard Scott segments, in which he showcases the photographs of viewers celebrating their 108th birthdays.

- "ROSEANNE." Take heart knowing that once your baby is born, Roseanne and Dan Connor will still look like that and you won't.

- RERUNS OF "IRONSIDES" AND "JAKE AND THE FAT MAN." For obvious reasons.

- ANY RICHARD SIMMONS INFOMERCIAL. Put the TV on mute, then just sit back with a carton of Häagen-Dazs. Enjoy.

SEXLESS BLOB MOOD

At this time you may also experience severe doubts about your sexuality. Does your husband still find you desirable? (You're not even sure you *want* him to find you desirable, but that's beside the point.)

It's hard to feel comfortable about sex when you're wearing someone else's body. Even after primping and dolling yourself up with perfumes and negligees, you still may feel like a drag queen tag-team wrestler. ("She's got him in a half nelson and finishes him off with a body slam to the mat!")

Try acting out fantasies. Ask him how he feels about being seduced by a sumo wrestler. Has he ever dreamed about scaling the Matterhorn? How about some belly bucking, big boy? (wink, wink)

Actually, researchers report that many men find women to be at their most sexually attractive during pregnancy. Of course, these are the same men whose eyewitness reports constitute the bulk of the world's UFO sightings.

Nevertheless, there's a body of thought that holds that pregnancy is a wonderfully sensual experience. In fact, certain members of the academic world have noted that even *labor and delivery* can be a Profoundly Sexual Experience. (Author's note: Put down that gun! Look, I just report this stuff, OK???!)

Of course, these academics are not speaking of any labor or delivery they *themselves* have personally experienced. Clearly they are relying on unsubstantiated hearsay found on the walls of lavatory stalls in state hospitals for the criminally insane.

One particularly unbalanced individual who

shall remain nameless (so that pregnant women cannot track him down and stuff cat hair down his throat) draws eleven points of comparison between sexual excitement and actual childbirth.

He points out such startling similarities as a change in breathing, tendency to make vocal noises, and facial expressions suggestive of an athlete under great strain.

Of course the same things can be observed in persons who are drowning.

Even attempting to open a stubborn jar of *mayonnaise* can produce these symptoms.

Researchers conveniently overlook the 1,792 dramatic *differences* between sexual excitement and childbirth, which include placentas and episiotomies.

14
Ask Ms. Preggers

Questions from the Expectant Mother

Dear Ms. Preggers,
My doctor has told me that the purplish red lines on my thighs are perfectly normal, but I'm not convinced. They look awful! What are they?

You must understand that anything that does not have an insurance billing code is "perfectly normal." That does not mean they *look* normal.

Your doctor may have told you that they are telangiectases, which is Latin for "ugly red lines that have no insurance billing code." Your doctor may also have mentioned that they will go away in time, which is his way of telling *you* to go away for a time.

The best you can do is try to camouflage them. With fine-line markers, sketch in an intricate design that lends itself to the pattern of your lines—a schematic of the New York subway system is good.

Dear Ms. Preggers,

Ever since I became pregnant, I cannot stand the smell of my husband's cologne. I've explained to him how this affects me, but he insists on wearing it. Is there anything I can do?

Saltine crackers are the expectant mother's all-purpose secret weapon against nausea and are exceptionally effective against this sort of olfactory assault. Just crumble up two or three and stuff them in his cologne bottle. Keep an extra handful handy for his shorts.

Dear Ms. Preggers,

I've heard that unborn babies can communicate while they're still in the uterus. Is this true?

Absolutely. Doctors at AT&T have discovered that the umbilical cord is, in fact, a phone line. (Why do you think they named the phone company Ma Bell?) Using the mother's navel as a phone jack, you merely hook up the Preggophone and dial in. ("Hello? Listen, you little twerp, *get off* my bladder.")

Can fetal voice mail be far behind? ("Hi. This is your bundle of joy. I've stepped out of the womb for a moment. . . .")

Ms. Preggers suggests you block outgoing 900 calls from the womb and obtain an unlisted phone number to discourage telephone solicitors.

Dear Ms. Preggers,

This is supposed to be the happiest time of a woman's life. My ankles are swollen, my

*back hurts, I have hemorrhoids, my
hair's falling out, I cry all the time, and
I'm exhausted. What am I doing wrong?*

From your symptoms, it sounds to Ms. Preggers
that everything's going precisely according to plan!

*Dear Ms. Preggers,
    I know about some of the different child-
birth theories—Childbirth Without Fear,
Childbirth Without Pain—but are there any
others I should know about?*

Yes. *Fear Without Childbirth:* Mother-to-be reads
a horror novel that scares the stuffing out of her and,
hopefully, the child. Also, *Pain Without Childbirth,*
wherein the mother's pubic area is prepped with an
Epilady, after which she is declared to be experiencing only false labor and is then sent home.

*Dear Ms. Preggers,
    I am just starving all the time! How can a
little baby possibly make me eat so much?*

Prepregnancy, your visits to buffets proved that
your eyes were bigger than your stomach. Now—unless you are Liza Minnelli—your eyes are consider-
ably smaller than just about everything, especially
your appetite.
    It takes more than 85,000 calories, in addition to
the ones needed for your own nutrition, to have a
healthy baby. Your body, unfortunately, does not
grasp the concept that this is a *cumulative* total, not
a *daily* requirement. So it will think you're playing
Deal-a-Meal with three decks.

Dear Ms. Preggers,

My cravings are driving me nuts! One day I'm a raving maniac in desperate search of Triscuits with peanut butter and mushrooms; the next it's a panic attack over sardines! No two days are alike. What can I do?

Milk the situation. People are dying to be able to do something for you. Remember when they said, "If you ever need anything, don't be afraid to pick up the phone?" Well, go ahead and do it. When you're seized with a craving for hot wings with butterscotch sauce, dial 'em up.

Make sure, however, that your craving strikes onlookers as a true craving. BE SPECIFIC. If you call them up at three A.M. and say you feel like milk and cookies, a sense of urgency is lacking. No, to qualify as an authentic craving, it should be more along the lines of a plea for a ten-ounce glass of ice-cold, 2 percent Borden Dairy Brand with exactly eleven Pepperidge Farm Lady Fingers dipped in chocolate and eight Toll House Cookies, freshly baked, still gooey from the oven.

Dear Ms. Preggers,

I will be going back to work shortly after the baby is born and will need to use a breast pump for feedings. Do you have any suggestions?

There are several different kinds of breast pumps, ranging in sophistication and price, but they all have one thing in common: you will feel like a complete jackass while using them. Before undertaking any such activity, be sure to invest in some good window shades.

The manual breast pumps look something like the horn on a youngster's trike. (Just as a point of reference, a breast pump does not go *honk-honk* or *ah-oo-ga ah-oo-gah*.) There are also motorized breast pumps that, if you don't mind feeling like a dairy cow, speed up the process. You will, however, look (and feel) as if you've been hooked up to a V-6 engine. The good news is, you could get up to eighteen miles per gallon.

> *Dear Ms. Preggers,*
> *I grew up on a farm, and all my life I've watched animals give birth. I think I know how it's done, and I see no reason I should have to go to class or to the hospital. I'll just do what comes naturally.*

Just because animals have a keen grasp of this does not mean you should mimic their techniques. Cats, for example, lick the mucus from their babies and eat the afterbirth. DO NOT DO THIS! This will be done for you in the hospital (which is one of the reasons they charge so much).

QUESTIONS FROM THE FATHER-TO-BE

> *Dear Ms. Preggers,*
> *My wife is pregnant, but I'm experiencing all the same symptoms—morning sickness, weight gain, mood swings, and food*

cravings. Is it normal for husbands to go through this?

This is an extremely common phenomenon. So common, in fact, that it has been given its own name—*couvade syndrome*. (There is an apparent shortage of appropriate foreign words available for syndromes, because *couvade* is French for "to hatch." Evidently there is no French word for "spousal attention-getting device.")

You and your wife are obviously acutely attuned to each other; your symptoms can be attributed to your empathy for your wife, which is very touching, albeit highly annoying. However, the morning sickness you are experiencing is just your body's normal reaction to having to observe your wife ralphing all over the pillow at seven A.M. You can alleviate your morning sickness by eating saltine crackers in a location such as, oh, across the street.

Although couvade syndrome is very common, that does not mean it is normal. It is, in fact, extremely weird, and you should not breathe a word of it to your buddies at the gym, especially if your symptoms include a need for a 38DD cup.

Dear Ms. Preggers,

It's hard for me to truly understand what a woman goes through when she's going through labor. Do you have any suggestions for what I can do to get a better grasp of the experience so I can be more empathetic and supportive? ·

Certainly. Merely place your head into a Thigh-Master as a well-muscled assistant squeezes and releases. Repeat every three minutes for twelve to twenty-four hours.

Or, using a nutcracker, think of your testicles as a pecan.

Dear Ms. Preggers,
Although I've gone through the birthing classes with my wife, I'm concerned that when the time comes I will panic and forget everything. Is this something to be worried about?

Yes. Obsess over it at every opportunity. Brood. Develop stomach ulcers. Not only will you panic and forget everything; you may well become a quivering mass of Jell-O and make a fool of yourself in the process. Mercifully, you will be wearing a surgical mask to conceal your identity.

Actually, regardless of how you conduct yourself, the baby *will* be born and, with all the commotion, is unlikely to notice what a doofus you are.

Dear Ms. Preggers,
I'm afraid that after the baby is born my wife's body will be a real turnoff—all fat and flabby and loose and rearranged. What can I do to keep her from going to pot?

May I assume from your question that *you* look like Steven Seagal? I didn't think so.

Rarely does Ms. Preggers come across such a touching display of concern and tenderness. Unfortunately, Ms. Preggers does not have any suggestions on how to help your wife avoid losing her figure. She does, however, have a few pointed observations for your wife regarding some other things she should consider losing. (You are very thoughtful to want to help your wife keep her figure, since it will help her to have confidence as she starts dating again after the divorce.)

Dear Ms. Preggers,
I'm told that newborns don't look very attractive when they're born, and I want to be prepared for this. What should I expect?

All newborns look like Winston Churchill, Walter Matthau, or Sammy Davis, Jr., without the well-formed heads. The head, of course, is shaped like a sweet potato.

Dear Ms. Preggers,
My wife acts as if I don't know the first thing about what she'll be going through. Having passed a kidney stone once, I know what pain is. It's pretty much the same, right?

Unless you passed the Blarney Stone or the Hope Diamond, NO.

Glossary

Pregnancy has its own unique vocabulary. By virtue of simply *being* pregnant, expectant mothers are presumed to be conversant in all the terms and terminology. As it happens, Preggese is not offered as a foreign language elective course in most schools, so, as experienced preggos bandy about the lingo, you'll feel left out, lacking the necessary vocabulary skills to participate, a wallflower in the dance hall of gestation.

But now you too can join in the gabfests and amaze your friends with your extensive knowledge.

With the following tutorial, written in easy-to-understand language, you no longer need to fear looking like a doofus when the conversation turns to topics you know nothing about. Simply adopt a thoughtful expression, nod knowingly, and interject one of these tidbits of revelation.

For example, should the term *preeclampsia* come

up, you'll be ready with the following witty observation: "Ah, yes, the art museum has a wonderful display of Etruscan urns from that period. Preeclampsia, I believe."

See how easy this is? Now, pay attention, ladies.

Apgar Score—Scale on which Olympic judges rate the newborn on style, execution, and technical difficulty of its dismount from the uterus.

Amniocentesis—A malarialike illness caused by giant tropical mosquitoes who feed on the amino acids of its victims.

Analgesics—Painkillers for hemorrhoids.

Areola—Saturday morning cartoon superhero from the planet Booberon in the center of the Milky Way. Resembles Madonna.

Bilirubin—Famous song writer ("Yellow Submarine," "Yellow Rose of Texas," and "Tie a Yellow Ribbon").

Braxton-Hicks—Wide receiver from the University of Alabama, winner of the Heisman Trophy, known for his fakes while carrying.

Breech presentation—So termed for the breech of etiquette involved as baby arrives mooning the birth attendant.

Cervix—Overnight courier service company for when it absolutely, positively has to be delivered overnight.

Chloasma—Facial discoloration and asthma-like itchy, watery eyes, such as that which occurs when watching performances by actress Cloris Leachman.

Colostrum—Tourist attraction in mountainous region of ancient Rome famous for its leaking aqueducts. (No connection to Norwegian dairy farmer Olaf Colostrum.)

Demerol—Gasoline additive that will have your engine purring.

Dilation—The mixed emotions experienced while going through labor and delivery. ("I want to DIE . . . but I'm so HAPPY.")

Effleurage—Lamaze technique of stroking the belly, inspired by Effie LeRouge and her trained poodles.

Epidural—In Greek mythology, the goddess of deliverance; daughter of Morphine, wife of Deadenus.

Episiotomy—A surgical incision intended to enlarge a woman's opening during childbirth, from the Greek *epis*, meaning "to appease" and *otomy*, meaning "Get this baby OUTTA ME!"

Fallopian tubes—Route the egg must travel to get to the uterus. First mentioned in the epistles (II Fallopians: 13-22); "Go forth and travel ye therefore, bringing tidings of great joy and, on occasion, big surprises."

Fetus—MTV cartoon character Beavis's baby brother.

Forceps—Enlarged muscle groups found on the forearms of pregnant bodybuilders.

Friedman Curve—Standard scale for the stages of labor; not to be confused with Dead Man's Curve.

Kegel exercises—Calisthenics for the bladder; developed by students at campus keggers.

Lactation—A dance popularized in the sixties by Little Eva. ("A chug-a chug-a motion that's so easy to do now . . . c'mon baby, do the lac-a-ta-tion . . .")

Lanugo—The fine, downy hair that covers newborns, named for South Dakota's own Lanugo twins, who, at the age of seventeen, made their way into the *Guinness Book of World Records* for their record-breaking use of 432 bottles of Nair in a single academic year.

Lightening—What pregnant women do to their mustaches.

Linea Nigra—Caribbean island nation located below the equator.

Mastitis—Inflammation of the milk glands that causes a mastodonlike disposition in its sufferers.

Meconium—Active ingredient in atomic bombs and baby poop.

Moro Reflex—The startle response exhibited by infants when hearing a loud noise or when moved suddenly. So named for television journalist Edward R. Murrow, whose interview techniques first elicited this reaction during the McCarthy hearings.

Perineum—Area on a theater stage located between the two exits.

Pitocin—High-performance fuel additive developed by Indy car racer Pete Pitocin to speed things up. "Gentleman, start your engines!"

Placenta—Madrid's best-known bed-and-breakfast resort, favorite retreat of the Infanti family, with reputed ties to the Umbilicus brothers.

Postpartum—Breakfast cereal for new mothers. Won't get soggy in milk.

Quickening—The rapid sprinting motion made by relatives when the mother feels the baby kicking. "Quick! Get in here! You gotta feel this!"

Transition—The most intense stage of labor, so called because of the changes a woman undergoes. (See *The Exorcist* for details.)

Uterus—Real estate development company specializing in efficiency apartments with emphasis on term leases for furnished wombs. ("No pets. Children OK.")

Vernix—The greasy coating covering baby at birth, named for Verna Mae Nixon of Memphis, Tennessee, who went her entire sophomore year without bathing.